DEDICATION

I dedicate this book to those Jamaicans who in the late 1950s fought hard so that I could walk the streets with dignity and in greater safety.

Roy Smith

ACKNOWLEDGEMENTS

I am very grateful to Arif Ali who has decided to publish this book and those helpful Hansib staff in the layout and typesetting department. My eternal gratitude to Jenny Lawther and John Hughes for their encouragement, their sound advice and skills without which this book would not have been possible.

Roy Sawh

UK—a black hole for Blacks

By A Staff Reporter

NEW DELHI, May 17.

FORTY-SIX years old Mr Roy Sawh, co-founder of Free University for Black Studies in London, is in India to canvass support for a "black movement" in Britain triggered by the "racist laws."

When he says black he means all the three million coloured people living in Britain.

He argues with passion the case for the coloured people in Britain. "Swamping of culture" was how Mrs Margaret Thatcher, the British Prime Minister, referred to the problem of coloured people's immigration to her country. But Mr Sawh feels that very soon she may find herself swamped with strong pressures from a Third World lobby being formed in Britain with the people of African, Carribean and Asian origin joining hands.

Mr Sawh said an Afro-Caribbean-Asian conference was being held in London on June 29. The various immigrants' associations would be invited to form a national body to fight for justice to the coloured people of Britain.

A tenacious and fiery anti-racist, he argues, "If we get organised we can have a lobby like the Jews in the United States. We can be a Third World lobby for trade, aid and development.

VIRGINITY TESTS

Talking about the much debated virginity tests on coloured women immigrants, he said, "They are still being continued." He claimed that X-ray tests were also being carried out on the coloured immigrants to determine their age and asked, "If this is what is happening to Asians in Britain, what is the Indian government doing about it?"

He said the immigrant organisations were now demanding the resignation of Mr David Lane, chairman of Commission for Racial Equality, ex-Tory minister. "We want a chairman for the coloured, above all a woman heads the Equal Opportunity Commission and the Arts Council. The Commission case tells us that it is not...

solve our problems — it is only there to give us guidelines.

He spoke with some anger when he talked of the double standards being adopted by the British government. He said, "When the white man comes to our country he's called the settler. And when we go to his country he calls us an immigrant.

a single member in the British Parliament, not even a single full time judge. There were not many of the 90 seats in Parliament were reserved for the Whites who hardly constituted even a fraction of the population.

Flaying the British TV and the Press for "biased coverage of India", he said the way they presented news one would imagine that India had only "other Teresa and starvation to offer." With discernible resentment, he added, "They have no respect for our countries—that is why we are having difficulties in race relations."

He also singled out organisations like Oxfam which he said were giving India a very bad reputation abroad. He said, "Posters of Indians with begging bowls were pasted all over the underground railway stations in London, asking for donations. They put emphasis on starvation as though India has nothing else to offer. They should know that India is one of the most industrialised nations in the world and self-sufficient in many spheres. It is also a leading non-aligned nation in the international community."

...also complained of eco-...ties between the white ...ed people in Britain. ...a young immigrant ...people who ...quer. If, for ...per week ...figure ...you ...n.

RACIALISM IN UK

Black leader calls for retaliatory action

By A Staff Reporter

"The only way to teach the British authorities a lesson is to subject the first English woman who comes to Delhi airport to a virginity test."

Drastic methods, definitely — but this is all that will really shake the wits out of their racial tendencies, says Roy Sawh, a prominent black leader in the UK.

Indian, whose father migrated to Guyana, Roy spent his early years there, and then went to London to become one of the well-known Hyde Park speakers and the first to raise their voice against discriminatory treatment of blacks living there.

According to Roy, racism in Britain was becoming worse for it was getting "institutionalised". It has filtered down from the Government to all areas of the local authorities and the police...

...is there for anybody to see... ...that it might not be long... ...there is an open street... ...and street, violence breaks out... ...much wider scale than ever...

...police, he said, had begun ...more and more blacks ...Suspicion Law, more ...the police the right to ...of anyone, search ...the next year, detained were ...in to 40 per cent, as figure ...ons protested loudly, blacks ...constitute the bulk of ...population, 15 per ...blacks on ...ding of

has met the Home ...ernment support as he...
build up

Ray Sawh

CONTENTS

INTRODUCTION
By Rev. Rudy Mohammed .... Page 9

PART ONE
ROY SAWH, A PROFILE
By Lionel Morrison .... Page 18

PART TWO
"FROM WHERE I STAND"
By Roy Sawh, 1980 .... Page 58

BLACK POWER IN BRITAIN
Roy Sawh .... Page 78

EPILOGUE
By Dr David Dabydeen .... Page 93

Introduction

By Rev. Rudy Mohammed

Roy Sawh's story contains all the elements of the life story of any black Westindian in Britain. The ambitions, the hopes, the frustrations and bitterness are all there. Roy's is by no means a success story. No black Westindian in Britain can boast of a truly successful story. There is always a missing ingredient, an unfulfilled hope.

The "Black Monster" who now confronts the Englishman on his own home ground is the creation of colonial rule. Colonial education taught him to despise his blackness and his race. Arnold Toynbee, the British historian, describes the systematic dehumanisation of the black man when he describes how the 'white' dominant minority denied the negro's humanity by the assertion of his (a) religious nullity – the black man's religious forms, rituals and expression were snatched from him and condemned as 'devilish'; (b) by the assertion of his cultural nullity – his cultural forms were branded as primitive, pagan and backward; (c) by the assertion of his political and economic nullity: he was too primitive, too stupid, too backward to have any political or economic sense; and (d) by the assertion of his racial inferiority and nullity as a human being – he was regarded as not being fully human but rather more of a primate in the process of development to full humanity.

The black man was left with nothing, stripped naked in his own eyes and in the eyes of the society which dominated him. This denial of the black man's human dignity was not an overt education but a subtle assumption and assertion which was endemic in the fabric of society of the dominant 'white' minority. Is it any wonder then, that many of the former colonies of the once British Empire have severed the political umbilical cord from the 'Mother' country in bitterness and even rebellion? Can one fail to understand then, the restlessness, the confusion and the apparent contradiction of the black man?

Denuded and left bare, there was need to fill the vacuum thus created. This was taken care of by the overt educative process. The black Westindian was taught that everything good, desirable, wholesome, true and just was to be found in Britain among the British and in British society. Roy Sawh boasts of his good colonial education. He knew all about English history, English heroes and even England itself. "The English were good teachers", he says, "and we were good students". As Roy remarked, and as many an ex-colonial black man in Britain today will assert, there was no reason then to disbelieve the colonial masters. They were "rather decent chaps" in the colonies. So England became the Mecca wherein the black Westindian could find 'salvation'. It was there that he would recover the fullness of his human dignity; that his self-esteem would be restored. It was not poverty, or starvation or overcrowding which drove Westindians to Britain. Many of them left lands, estates and good jobs behind. It was that deep-seated yearning to be 'somebody'; a full human person equal to any other and accepted as such which was the motivating force. No wonder Roy was "all cock-a-hoop" as he prepared to sail from his native Guyana for England.

Another aspect of the colonial system which contributed to the deep aspiration for salvation among the Westindian masses was the socio-economic system. Roy's reminiscences of the pressure he faced in his youth; of having to grow up overnight, of having to help around the house to look after his younger brothers and sisters, to cultivate a 'kitchen garden' and to go fishing in order to supplement the meagre wage of a hard working father; this was a normal way of life among the disadvantaged working classes. The socio-economic system in colonial Guyana, as in the rest of colonial Westindies, did not make life easy for those at the bottom of the social ladder. Nor did it easily offer a way out. The slogan that one must work hard in order to achieve success must have seemed a farce as black citizens watched their parents work themselves to exhaustion, as Roy watched his, and saw no hope of any kind of success; no just recompense for their labour. Today the black man is said to be lazy, irresponsible and unreliable. Perhaps it is because he no longer believes that hard work brings just rewards – at least, not for the black man. Roy Sawh turned his back on work on the plantation and found gambling less arduous and far more rewarding. Britain was portrayed as the land of opportunity; the land of social mobility; the land in which the streets were paved with gold. More than any other country in the world, the colonial black man aspired to travel to England. Can one blame him?

It was therefore a real culture shock when Westindians, full of hopes, dreams and fantasies, stepped off the boat train at Victoria Station in London to face the reality of British society. Roy Sawh says he could not believe that he was really in London. It was necessary for him to seek confirmation from a policeman. He could not envisage white folk performing the menial tasks which he assumed were reserved for black people like himself. The myth of an England of royalty and aristocrats, of gentlemen and ladies of elegance, politeness and fine manners were shattered by the stark reality. His good colonial education did not prepare him to expect a class, at the bottom of English society, of white people who were no better off, culturally, intellectually, economically or politically than the black working classes at home. He was even more shocked, as he recalled, when he realised that another rung was being created further down the social ladder to fit in all the blacks who were flocking to Great Britain.

When the evil head of racial discrimination really and finally struck home, the result was shattering. All the cherished hopes and dreams of a new beginning for the dehumanised black man evaporated. The reaction produced three different responses. There were those who decided that accommodation was better than nothing. The saying 'if you can't lick them, then join them,' was seen as the way out. Without an identity or a history of their own, some black people in Britain accommodate themselves to the society and culture of the English. They accept the values and standards of the host society, attach themselves to 'safe' white friends and in this close-circuit, insulated world they 'pretend' that there is no prejudice. They really do not see any racism because they do not allow themselves to see it. They prefer to enjoy some semblance of their dreams rather than be crushed by the reality.

Then there are those who withdraw into a world of depression. Theirs is a world in which there is a total lack of interest in the life around them – civic, social or otherwise. Indeed, there is even a lack of interest in life itself. The population at the mental institutions in Britian are well represented by members of this group. Then there are those who hit back; those who angrily reject the treatment meted out to themselves. They are the ones who are articulate, militant, are organisers and leaders of movements for rights and justice. They vent their rage in vitriolic language against British society and start numerous half-hearted movements. The fact is they do not really know how to handle the situation. Roy Sawh was one of this group.

Roy's oratory at Hyde Park drew large numbers of black people because, as he himself realised, he was echoing in impeccable English, so that the Englishman must understand, what every black man was feeling deep down in his heart. In his harangue, Roy does not always adhere to the rigorous laws of logic. He makes statements that are vague, assumptions that are untested, analogies that are not necessarily true, but logical dissertation is not his interest. He is communicating the anger, the frustration, the bitterness which the black Westindian feels, and he does that well.

Many an attempt was made to organise the black people in Britain and to create a united front. There is strength in unity. Organisations were formed, were enthusiastically received initially, performed creditably for a while but then fell by the wayside. It was a pattern that was to be repeated many times. Somehow, black unity remained an elusive dream.

Roy Sawh recalls, with a degree of nostalgia, some such attempts. The Universal Coloured Peoples' Association (UCPA) was widely acclaimed by both 'black' and 'white', but eventually went the way of all flesh. Roy advances a number of reasons which he thought contributed to the unhappy demise of such a promising organisation. He cites his own reputation as a militant and extremist as not being helpful. The disparity in the social, political and economic backgrounds of the rank and file did not help either. He speaks of nit-picking over rules and constitutions, of the lack of direction, of being lionised by white liberals. These were some of the many reasons which contributed to the eventual death of the UCPA.

When the Racial Adjustment Action Society (RAAS) was formed, an attempt was made to avoid all these errors. RAAS was more homogeneous, had a positive programme and direction, and refused the helpful hands of white liberals. But after an effective and hopeful beginning, RAAS, too, came to an end. This time, Roy indicates, the problem was the difference in ideologies in the leadership.

He does not however, suggest any reasons for the passing away of the Free University for Black Studies, but he does mention, with some bitterness, the turncoat, even traitorous, attitude of many black people, former placard waving, demonstrating, militant activists, who suddenly lost all zeal for the black cause when they were offered jobs and positions – membership on fact-finding committees; the office of Justice of

From Where I Stand

the Peace, etc., – which seemed to imply recognition and acceptance by the white community; former militants who suddenly joined the ranks of accommodationists.

"In 1976", Roy recalls, "after a two-year absence from Britain, I came back to London and the whole black scene appeared to be in turmoil. The impact 'Black Power' had made on the British society appeared to have been curtailed, if not manipulated by the establishment. This I am sure was the work of the white liberals, and most of the black people who were involved in the Black Power movement had become 'social workers'. They had become employed by statutory bodies and instead of articulating Black Power, they had become safety valves for the system. Instead of representing the interests of the black community, they ended up defending their employers. By doing this, they were indirectly defending their job positions. The concept was and still is relevant to the black community. Without power, the black community would and could never solve their problems. Token appointments by either of the four political parties is an appeasement, not genuine concern for the solution. For black people who would and are aspiring to become Councillors and Members of Parliament, they should be warned that their presence alone is not enough, only their full participation at all levels will change the racism which has now become institutionalised. To my black brothers and sisters who really believe that they can change the British attitude regarding racism, then I would advise them to read British history and the attitudes of the whites against the blacks. There are many white people who don't even know that they are subconsciously racists."

Another cause for complaint was the apparent lack of support and solidarity from the Caribbean governments. Roy remembers, in the heyday of his Black Power activism, his experiences in the Westindies.

"I left Guyana nevertheless, a wiser person, and at that time there was a Black Power Conference being held in Bermuda and, as I was invited, I decided to attend. I also decided to visit the other Westindian territories. I didn't realise that I was so popular until I arrived in Trinidad where I was given exactly one day to stay. I was furious that a black country would only allow me to stay for one day. I went on to Grenada and, with some difficulty, was allowed to stay for five days. The next day at 9.00a.m. I was rudely awakened by a police inspector who told me that I was 'an undesirable', that I had to leave immediately. I was flabbergasted. I left Grenada for Barbados where I did not expect any trouble from the Immigration department, but I was in for a not so pleasant surprise. They did not even allow me to go through Immigration as a tourist or an in-transit passenger, but was politely told that I was only allowed to stay in order to get the next flight out. I booked my flight for Bermuda. With some money to spare, I thought I would have plenty of time to relax before the Black Power Conference started. It was when I arrived in Bermuda that I realised how infamous I had become. I could not land and I realised afterwards that British Immigration Officers were in control at the desks and my name was on a 'black list'. How ironical that I was prevented from attending a Black Power Conference in a black country by white officers because my name was on a 'black list'".

The lack of real identity, of culture, or a vision of destiny, must be contributing factors to this apparent inability of black peoples to come together in unity and solidarity. The other ethnic groups in Britain do not seem to suffer the same malady. There is an element of truth in all the reasons Roy put forward, but perhaps, there is something else. Perhaps the black Westindians in Britain, in spite of activity and rhetoric to the contrary, still cherish, deep in their hearts, the hope that one day they will be acceptable to the white community and will be accorded equal status. Because, in spite of the frustrations, the disappointments, the anger, the black man in Britain does not want to leave.

The flame of hope and confidence, faint though it may be, in the traditional image of the English as gentlemen of justice and fair-play, still lingers in the heart of the black man in Britain. No wonder so many lose their zeal for black causes when offered the hands of friendship by the white establishment. No wonder too, that so many who were formally 'convinced' and convincing proponents of this or that ideology, – of Marxism, Black Power, Black Muslim etc. – suddenly changed their tunes, and often their appearance, when given the opportunity to rub shoulders and chat amiably with white colleagues on committees and special assignments. In times of frustration and depression, ideologies often serve as a vehicle to channel anger.

From Where I Stand

Roy Sawh, Director of Black Rights (UK), an organisation that offers free legal advice and representation, listening to a salient point being made by Lord Scarman, Patron of Black Rights (UK). The organisation is based at 221 Seven Sisters Road, London N4. Tel: 01-281-2340

Part One

Roy Sawh

a profile

By Lionel Morrison

Chapter One

Every Sunday afternoon at Speaker's Corner in London, a small conventionally dressed black man from Guyana mounts the platform, surveys the crowd of people, mostly white, whom he fondly describes as a "raving bunch of lunatics", and begins to harangue his English hosts in impeccable English.

"Black Power is black pride. It is our way of freeing ourselves from white domination. Eveywhere the black man is on the march, Asia, Africa and Latin America. Two thirds of the world's population is on the move. We are not alone here." And then the coup de grace – "It's up to you whites to make the next move. The black man won't be shoved about any more."

Sometimes, he goes off at a tangent. "You Englishmen are so daft", he pronounces amiably, as though he were handing out a bouquet of flowers. "No wonder your girls prefer to go out with foreigners like me. When an Italian sees a girl he likes sitting in the park, he goes straight up to her and talks to her. When a black man sees a pretty girl in the streets he does the same. When an Englishman sees a girl", he pauses and grins warily, "he walks round and round in circles". From the whites a shower of appreciative chuckles falls lightly on the smooth afternoon air. The black people lap up his words.

Beneath the surface frivolity of his statements lurks a deep and permanent truth about the white anxiety regarding black sexuality which Roy casually exposes. As Professor Polarin Shyllon writes, "Black men marrying white women was, and is, the root of British racism."

Apart from his colour the Guyanese looks like a small, properly manicured English clerk trying to cut adrift from his working class origins. He wears dark tailored suits, plain white shirts and sombre ties, and he stares at the crowd through dark metal rimmed glasses. He draws the biggest crowd, is Hyde Park's foremost orator and one of Britain's well-known controversial Black Power leaders. This is a long haul for a man who some years ago stepped from an Italian boat at Southampton, penniless, with a limited education, and politically ignorant, who believed passionately in Queen and Motherland, and who had come to make enough money to return "within a few years" to Guyana a rich man.

Roy Sawh with his father, mother, daughters (L-R) Oma and Shashi and sister Cilla, 1971

>...when the Africans were fighting for their land in Kenya against the whites, the Africans were called Mau-Mau. When the Vietnamese were fighting for their land against the Americans, they were called Viet Cong. When the Palestinians are fighting for their land against the Zionists they are called Terrorists. When the Blacks in Rhodesia were fighting for their land against the Whites, they were called Guerillas: but when the French were fighting against the Germans for their land, they were called Resistance Fighters and when the Hungarians were fighting for their land against the Soviets, they were called "Freedom Fighters"...

Chapter Two

Roy Sawh was born on 11th January, 1934, on a big sugar estate in Uitvlugt, Guyana. The second eldest son in a family of six children Roy's history is typical of black people in the former colonies. His father was a sugar estate worker or "coolie" as they were called then, who was brought from India at the end of the 19th century to work on the sugar plantations in Guyana. Roy's mother was a second generation Guyanese whose family also came from India.

Their home was the typical poor plantation worker's bungalow: small, one-bedroom, a kitchen where all the daily activities took place and a medium sized sitting room in which the children slept on a few mats which disappeared into the cupboards during the day.

When Roy's elder brother turned twelve he went to live with a childless aunt and uncle, and Roy became the eldest with all the responsibilities that it involved. "It was like growing up overnight. There were all the things expected from the eldest in the house. I had to help in the house cleaning up, looking after my younger brothers and sisters. We had innumerable financial problems. My father got a weekly wage of £3 with which we just managed to keep alive. We had our own little garden which provided the vegetables which the £3 could not cover. I became an expert fisherman. One thing, there were plenty of fish."

Then there was school. Roy's mother was a fanatic about education. Determined not to let her children become "coolies", she would sacrifice all available pennies to ensure that he continued at school.

"She was marvellous, that woman. I don't know how she managed on that £3. She stretched it endlessly. We always had good food, but that was all. One shirt was replaced once in six months, after it had been patched and washed to threads."

At the age of sixteen, small and fragile, he reached the pinnacle of what could be offered..."I did not acquire any qualifications whatsoever. All I could do was to read and write in a fashion. I was ripe and ready for the labour market and since it was expected of me I became a labourer on the sugar estate. But my mother was not happy, she wanted me to try for further educational heights."

He was deeply affected by the inhumane, even obscene, behaviour of the white plantation overseers and this helped to shape his later vision of the relationship between the white and black people. "I remember, as a little boy, seeing a foreman of the 'cane cutters' gang, whose job was in jeopardy, having to take his daughter by night to the white overseer's house, and then having to wait outside the yard to collect her early next morning. Only through this enforced prostitution could he maintain his position. As a Hindu, the notion of family purity is an entrenched and supreme part of our ancestral culture, so that this act was a measure of our humiliation. These nocturnal acts were a common feature of life on the sugar estate."

Roy's mother was determined that he should be protected against such experiences, and made sure that he continued his education. This however cost money which meant that Roy's father had to work literally day and night – by day, he was a cane cutter, and by night, he was employed as a watchman.

The High School offered a kind of competition which led to a two-year scholarship. But it meant going to Georgetown, the capital, which was a new experience. Although it meant sleeping rough he was undeterred and so, stimulated by the thought of inner city life, he religiously went to the capital to participate in the competitions. He won a two-year scholarship for a three-year course, and also developed an appetite for those bright city lights which has never left him. Lack of money prevented him from completing his course.

His first job was an accountant's boy with the princely pay of twenty five shillings a week. It was a lot for a young man of 19 years in rural Guyana. "I remember that first week. My whole pay had to go to my grandmother as custom demanded. It was a matriarchal set-up which was very rigid. I resented giving her my hard-earned money. But what could you do?"

His first conflict with the establishment came when his boss was not happy with the quality of the white shirt he was wearing to work. "It was not white enough, not classy enough. I used to wash it at home every evening before going to bed. The creases used to come out whilst I was wearing it. It was a

From Where I Stand

time when drip dry shirts were available in the Caribbean." The boss wanted him to get a new shirt – half of his pay. So he lost his job and drifted into another and then onto the sugar estate again which was too much for him physically. "I quit. It was too difficult for me."

He tried to get a job in the civil service, but he failed because he was not a Christian. Hope of employment seemed to be in Georgetown and at the age of twenty he got a job as a delivery boy. It was hell trying to make a living. Pay was poor, accommodation was bad. It was during this period that he felt he had reached a loneliness as never before. Nothing seemed to go right. His ambitions looked thwarted. And then he turned to gambling with cards and dominoes. He earned more money than his father ever did. For three to four years life was good. There was money, there was food, there were clothes – good ones at that. Shirts he had only previously enjoyed looking at in shop windows were now his own. He had money for his family. "I dressed to kill and had plenty of money. I lived luxuriously." He knew it was wrong to make all that money gambling. It went against all the family training. But he had to survive.

It was through his mother's insistence that he gave up gambling and the easy way of making money. It was not easy. "I was not sure whether it was the right thing to do. But in Guyana when your mother engaged in battle, she always won. She was always right."

But if Roy had his personal problems, Guyana was in even bigger difficulties. 1953 was a time when one constitutional crisis was followed by another. The political atmosphere was tense and exciting. Cheddi Jagan had just won the elections and was threatening the status quo with his radicalism and militancy. The British colonial administrators sent in troops. "When the troops were brought in we knew that Jagan must have done something very bad against the Queen, our Queen, although she was thousands of miles away. People were friendly towards the troops and invited them in for coffee. Here for the first time white people were walking in the plantations and not rushing about in posh cars, even if they were in greens and khakis. I was very naive politically then and so were many of my friends.

"I knew absolutely nothing of politics, and did not care to know. I was too busy trying to make a living."

His next job, which changed the pattern of his life considerably and led him to England, was insurance. He became an agent. It was his best experience. He did surprisingly well. His worldly possessions increased to a motor cycle which made him mobile and thus available. "I was starting to smell success", he says.

But if success was round the corner, frustration was at the door. He could sell only to black people and of course they did not have the big money.

It was frowned on and unheard of for a black insurance agent even to try to sell to whites. "I was scared stiff to think about it. Yet at the same time I resented the limitations of my custom. Our class barriers were too rigid for me to think further than being frustrated. I did not understand the mechanics of class divisions although I accepted it all, like accepting my place in the insurance world to sell only to black people. That was the extent of my political awareness."

His boss at the Insurance Company talked to him about England. The possibilities of further education, of easy money, the glamour of Britain. He became obsessed with the idea of getting away from Guyana and joining the trek to the mother-country. "I was excited just thinking of getting to Britain. I had heard so much about the country. It was a forbidden place in my estimation, after all my only association with whites in Guyana was on a master-servant relationship. Here was I, off to the home of my boss. It also meant me rising in the estimation of my friends, and a step up the social ladder for my family. You can imagine I was all-cock-a-hoop."

Chapter Three

And so on a misty March Sunday in 1958 Roy Sawh arrived in Britain with the wonderful knowledge that he had come to "do well", and would soon return to Guyana a rich man and relieve his mother once and for all of the continual anxiety of where the next slice of bread would come from.

"I expected to return to Guyana within two or three years with bags of money and a world of knowledge. I could already envisage in my mind's eye the scenes on my return to Uitvlugt. "Tell us about the Houses of Parliament, Roy. The Queen? The Crown Jewels." I was not really afraid. Was I not knowledgeable with English and about English history? The Wars of the Roses. The Restoration. Good Queen Bess. The Thirty Years' War. I considered it part of my history as well. That's how I rationalised my coming to England."

His first shock in Britain, which he now regards in retrospect as a joke, was when he saw a white man – a porter – carrying luggage at Victoria main line railway station. He could not believe his eyes, and if that was real he did not believe that he was in London. "I had been brought up to regard such menial jobs as being above the white man. Only black people did that kind of work in Guyana. I was so flabbergasted that I went up to a bobby and asked him whether I was in London!"

More surprises were forthcoming when he saw the elderly white women cleaning and sweeping toilets as lavatory attendants. "I got scared at the enormity of the whole thing. It was something completely new to me."

The friend who was supposed to have met him at the station never turned up. Just as he was becoming worried and afraid, a Jamaican befriended him, listened to his story and took him to Riverside Road, Stoke Newington, to stay with him. "It was very natural, I felt, for a black man to approach me and befriend me. It was like back home. If a white man had approached me I would have been terrified."

So with thirty shillings in his pocket Roy became another resident in one of London's back streets. He was told to register at the Labour Exchange and after filling in some forms, and producing his passport he got unemployment benefit. "I could not understand it. Here was I looking for a job and then getting some money for not having a job. The only thing I could say was 'what a great country'. I did not have any hang-ups then about receiving dole, as I would now. I had not applied for it and at first I thought they must have made a mistake."

His first experience of racial discrimination came when he had to look for accommodation. Landladies had suddenly "let their room earlier" when they saw him after assuring him on the 'phone half an hour before that they had vacancies. "It is only now I know it was racism. At that time I thought it was my fault. Maybe I had not heard correctly. My English was probably not so good and they might have heard incorrectly. I did not mind. I thought I was the one who was in the wrong. I can see now why so many black people accept racism. They are prepared to make excuses and bend over backwards to people who practise racism. It is still part of an inferiority complex and the colonial mentality."

Jobs! He worked in a mat factory, which meant getting up very early for little money; in a hotel washing dishes, which was better because it meant free food, and then into the inevitable of Westindian jobs – London Transport. He was very happy as a bus conductor. So happy that he took a picture of himself in uniform and sent it home to his mother to show her that he was trying to establish himself. The pay was good and he calculated that with about £13 per week he would soon return to Uitvlugt a rich man. But things did not work out as planned. The second week on the buses an elderly white woman spat in his face and called him a "black bastard". He pushed her and had practically the whole bus at his neck. "That was the end of my association with London Transport. I resigned in disgust."

He was so disgusted and ashamed at leaving his job that he dared not write to his mother. "She would have sighed and said it was typical of me. It would seem as if I could not keep a job, especially one as good as a bus conductor. I felt as if I had let her down." Another job as a clerk followed. He spent weeks walking from factory to factory looking for that job. It was a pleasant job which he held for three years. For the first time he had time to spare and used it by enrolling at night school for a course in accountancy.

From Where I Stand

With plenty of time during weekends he used to visit "lively" spots in London...Piccadilly, St James' Park and Hyde Park, places which gave him entertainment and cost nothing. At Speaker's Corner, Hyde Park, he drifted towards the platform which had a black speaker who was a Communist Party member. "I saw this black chap with a C.P. banner and was intrigued. For the first time in my life I was going to see and listen to a live communist. It was exciting and something like forbidden fruit. In Guyana, according to folklore, communists were very bad. Little did I know the effect this experience would have on me."

As he listened to the speaker analyse society and its ills, he convinced me that he came from Guyana. "What he said seemed to apply so correctly to my country. He spoke of racism and colonialism and showed how the colonial powers like Britain were exploiting the colonies." This was his first introduction to a Marxist analysis of society.

The next Sunday he again hurried to Speaker's Corner and this time asked the speaker whether he could also speak. "I could not say a thing at first. Apart from being heckled, I was dumbstruck. Nothing seemed to come out from me. It was as if I was in shock. But worse still, I suddenly realised that I had nothing to say. I was humiliated." That Sunday, and everyday afterwards, he bought newspapers and started reading them greedily. He joined a library and read Colin Cross' book *The Fall of the British Empire* which described colonial exploitation in detailed form. This made a deep impact on him. "No other book shaped my thinking like Cross' book." A new horizon was opening for him. He met new friends at the classes he was attending at night school. "We used to discuss things, how we felt, what were our problems and experiences. I started for the first time to realise that our problems were all the same – difficulties in getting a job, accommodation and racism."

He could not understand why English people seemed so prejudiced, especially when he remembered how whites on the sugar estates – which they mostly owned – were concerned about black people, where they lived, the jobs they had. They seemed so reasonable then. He wondered whether it was because black people were now in their country, and were a threat to them, that they discriminated against them. "I did not know. It was new to me. I thought maybe we were in the wrong. I still could not analyse the reasons."

He read more books, and concentrated on those dealing with politics and economics. At about the same time his contacts among black people grew, and so did the realisation that there was a lot amiss in British society. He could sympathise and listen to complaints by his fellow black people, but could do nothing. "I felt I was powerless to do anything constructive. It was like a nightmare to me. But what could I do? I could see no answer and my vision was not clear enough to attempt anything. So the next best thing I did was to try to develop myself. That is, I wanted to know more about life. What made things go in a particular direction. I developed an insatiable appetite for reading. For asking questions, for listening." With this new lust for knowledge and information, his interest in accountancy sagged. He became more interested in public administration. "I had the vague idea that would help me in my relations with people."

During the summer more black people emerged into the open from their winter hibernation. Hyde Park and other public places once more became Roy's haunt. From the number of people who were congregating around his platform he realised that he was getting good at the game of public speaking. He gained more confidence and sensed the power that there was once you had the audience in your grasp. To maintain the interest of his audience he had to keep up with current events. He spent more time reading newspapers. He also cultivated a group of friends, mostly from the Westindies, but especially from Barbados. "They seemed to be around more often, interested and more articulate than other Westindians. Their discussions always seemed to end with the same conclusion – that black people were having a bad time in Britain and that it was the result of colour prejudice.

In 1961 he joied the British Guyana Freedom Association, which was Marxist in orientation. He was very pro-Moscow in philosophy. They discussed issues like independence in Guyana, which road Guyana was taking and whether violence was the only way out for Guyana. "Talks used to go on endlessly. They were very academic. We had plenty of time."

Then the next year he saw an advertisement in a Guyana paper in which Guyanese were offered scholarships to study in the Eastern European countries. Although he says that he was prepared to do anything to get a scholarship and in that way to get into university, it seems more likely that going to university was a secondary reason. The first was the opportunity to get to Moscow. It was a popular period for black people to go to the Eastern European countries. Offered a scholarship and given the choice of three East European universities, he chose Moscow. He left his job without giving notice. His excuse: "My values had changed. I was more interested in education and not material things."

Once he got to Moscow he settled in quickly. He became more popular, met students from other colonial countries and got to know more about their countries. Two weeks after his arrival at university he called on students to form an Afro-Asian group and promptly caused a furore with the suggestion. The purpose, according to him, was for students to get to know each other better, to discuss the conditions in their countries and how to act collectively. "But I did not realise that I was indirectly challenging the establishment in Moscow. They did not like anything to be formed without their prior permission and active involvement."

From then onwards things did not go very smoothly between him and the Soviet university authorities. Black students started to complain about racial discrimination. "This was something new to me. I could well understand racism in a capitalist country like Britain. But a socialist country like the Soviet Union was the last place I expected any. I could not get over this. The whole thing interested me. I started asking a crucial question. Was there any real difference between Soviet socialism and Western capitalism? The answer to that is there even today in his views of the Soviet role in world politics, which are often sharply critical.

His next confrontation was during a seminar on international affairs at the university. A Soviet official spoke on the Congo. Roy says he was convinced that the official was twisting facts to suit the Soviet position. "I knew something about the situation in the Congo, having taken an active part in the various pro-Congo activities in London. All the official said was contrary to what I knew to be the situation. It was racist talk." He started to ask embarrassing and leading questions. "People realised that he was either not telling the truth or he did not know what he was talking about. The lecturer and I ended up in an argument. I hit the desk and walked out. I wasn't going to sit there, after all my experiences of racism in Britain, and listen to all that nonsense about my brothers and sisters in the Congo."

The next day he was called before his professor and told that his behaviour was unbecoming. He was also told that by walking out and thumping the desk he showed a lack of courtesy. "I had to rebuke him", he says. "Did Nikita Kruschev not thump the rostrum at the United Nations so hard with his shoe that his wristwatch broke? Surely that was not discourtesy, it was a way of lodging a protest. The professor was very annoyed. I think mainly because he had not known that Kruschev behaved like that at the U.N." It seems more likely that the professor was annoyed at Roy drawing a parallel between his (Roy's) behaviour and that of the leader of the mighty Soviet Union.

Racial discrimination increased on the campus. Roy organised the student leaders and together they brought the students out on strike, boycotting the lectures and the canteen.

"I am reluctant to talk about that period. But I think that it was an important phase in my life. It made me more sceptical about strict Marxist philosophy when propounded by whites."

There was the Larrisa incident. Apparently a black student married a Russian girl, took her to Africa and then, it was alleged, sold her to some chiefs who abused her. The girl it seems "staggered naked to the Soviet Embassy" and reported what had happened to her. She was then sent back to Moscow. This story was doing the rounds in Moscow with disastrous effects for black-white relations.

A deterioration in the relations between black and Russian students resulted. Black students were beaten up by Soviet "teddy boys" and the Ghanaian government stopped sending students to that particular university in Moscow. "It was a cold war period, and the Soviet authorities were not lifting a finger to put a stop to these happenings. "Things got so bad that you felt that every ordinary Russian in the street saw every black man as a direct descendant of a monkey who was still in that primitive stage of development."

Offensive articles appeared in the newspapers of the Komsomol – the Young Communist League. Roy was called to the Ghana High Commission and asked to drop his campaign. "I refused. How could I forget the whole thing, when I was studying there and was going to be there for the next five or six years? But his estimation was wrong. The Soviet authorities cabled Cheddi Jagan's office in Georgetown, Guyana, and the reply was that they must expel him. He refused to go voluntarily and was physically put on a 'plane to London and told "not to come back again". They even packed his luggage for him.

"That was the sum total of my studies in Moscow and brought to an abrupt end my sympathy for the Soviet Union and all it stands for – which I realised was no different from the abuses of capitalism. It was a year of great education for me. It made me rethink my attachment to Soviet Communist orthodoxy as I could not see how I could reconcile it to my blackness. The answer to racial discrimination did not lie there, I analysed." Thus ended his short-lived flirtation with Soviet Communism.

So where did that leave Roy politically? "I did not reject Marxism as such", Roy is eager to explain, "but I discarded Soviet Communist orthodoxy and dogmatism. I accept much of the economic and political analysis of Marxism, but I passionately believe that Marxism alone cannot deal adequately with all the problems faced by black people in this society. The answer must come from within the black community itself and from its actual experiences." So back in London he once again became the Hyde Park orator. But this time with a difference. He needed a political base.

Chapter Four

The Political and Economic Planning Report of 1965 showed the extent of discrimination against black people in this country. This report had a profound effect on Roy. "I was appalled, shocked and realised that not only was something wrong, but that something had to be done. This was different from other times when I had always known that something was wrong, but never went further to realise that something had to be done. At home when things were wrong, you always left it to the colonial administration – the whites – to put things right."

He invited some black friends to a discussion at his place. "This was a significant step for me. I was actually taking matters into my own hands in London." Many more meetings followed, some ending in arguments, others going late into the night. The prevailing feeling was that all the problems which black people were facing in this country were as a result of their disunity, so there had to be, at the onset, unity at all cost. "We knew that there was discrimination and we knew that there was no unity. So we concluded that all our problems would be solved if we were united."

The result of all these discussions was the formation of the Universal Coloured Peoples' Association (UCPA). Roy became interim Chairman. The organisation received a lot of publicity – good and bad. "We were primarily concerned with organising our people. We had a lot of publicity because it was a new organisation and the first of its kind. But it was not the type of publicity that helped us. Maybe it was the rhetoric that we used and the way I would deal with people publicly on the platform which was different from how I would handle people privately. I had the reputation of being a militant and an extremist.

This did not help our organisation. Of course there were problems. We were not a homogeneous group. We were black people from different parts of the world with different social, political and economic backgrounds. We then set up a committee to draw up a constitution with all the trappings of the constitutional parties in Britain."

It was during this period that he heard of Michael X, another black leader in London, who was then still known as Michael de Freitas. Michael X was appearing in the papers where he was talking on the same lines of black unity. Roy had talks with him.

An event then took place which helped to radically change his entire political thinking. Black American leader Stokely Carmichael arrived in Britain. "I spent a whole week with him, shared the platform with him. I talked to him, listened to him and was tremendously impressed with him. His ability to grasp a problem and then analyse it in detail, find a solution and then take steps to implement that solution was what really impressed me. There is no doubt that we were influenced by events in the USA and how our black brothers there were meeting the situation. We found that we were talking about more or less the same thing. But his solutions to the problems were not mine, mostly because at that time I was not sufficiently politically aware, and was not radical enough to realise that he was advocating certain very fundamental changes in society. I was nearly on the same wavelength as he, but needed a jolt here and there to complete my metamorphosis. I still had not grasped Black Power and all it meant. He set me on the road to it."

Although the UCPA was growing in membership, it was lacking in direction and programme. The leaders were being caught up in a personality cult and this caused a lot of resentment among the members, who accused the leadership of always appearing on TV, in the press and on radio. "We were being lionised by white liberals who started offering help and advice. Some black people had never been in such a situation before. From being outcasts to loverboys had to have its toll. And it did. There was a lot of vying for the attention of these liberals, which was what they wanted. I became very worried about the UCPA. It had potential but there was something else lacking. Black people were joining but were not getting the type of unity in terms of concise political action. Every time the question of action came up, we were arguing and fighting among ourselves. This was what the white liberals wanted."

Sybil Phoenix MBE presenting a friendship award to Roy Sawh

L-R: Brother George (Student Non-Violence Co-Ordinating Committee S.N.C.C. USA), Michael X (Racial Adjustment Society – RAAS), Stokely Carmichael (S.N.C.C.), Roy Sawh and Obi Egbuna (Universal Coloured People's Association – UCPA)

From Where I Stand

Roy then decided to go and consult Stokely who was by this time in Paris, after being refused re-entry into Britain on the completion of his African tour. "As chairman of the U.S. Student Non Violent Co-ordinating Committee and with his wide experience, we hoped that Stokely could let us have the benefit of his experience in dealing with similar situations. We talked for hours and it was during this period that the cause and trouble of our difficulties became clear to me. Whenever we formed black organisations we were influenced by the methods used by the oppressors. We tried to play their game. We modelled ourselves after them and because we had a different outlook to things we got entangled. In relation to black organisations it meant we became obsessed with such things as constitutions and all the restrictions they had on one's activity.

"You might argue that constitutions are important as a safeguard against a one man show, but then one man shows happen whether you have one or not. If you wanted to take political action on something, it meant getting a two-thirds majority. You had to call a meeting and by that time the problem would have disappeared or you had found there was no solution. Western democracy is a game and a luxury – a luxury that black people cannot afford. The constitutions are the rules of the game and the people who invented the game also invented the rules and once you invent the rules you are bound to win. So, I argued, why not invent our own game and our own rules? This meant that when the question of a constitution came up at a meeting of the UCPA, Roy forcefully argued against one. He argued for a programme with aims and objectives spelled out, but not a formal constitution. His ideas were not welcomed by the rest of the meeting. Instead of fighting and standing his ground, he walked angrily out of the meeting. "I was young and inexperienced and behaved irrationally and walked out. I regretted it afterwards. Here was something I had pioneered. It was my idea. It was my baby. It had come at the right time. I should have fought to the last and maybe even compromised if it meant playing an important role in the organisation. But my leaving left the field open to others who were too attached to the western way of running organisations. It was from this time onwards that I became a Black Power advocate."

He made contact with Michael X, later called Malik, who was just about to form his own black organisation. They had discussions for weeks and finally decided to go ahead with

Abdulla Patel, Jan Carew, the Guyanese writer, and others in forming the organisation. One thing which they were all clear about was that there would be no constitution, only a programme of objectives and aims. This was in fact a restatement of the rights of black people in Britain and how they hoped to achieve them.

The multi-racial approach of other organisations like CARD (The Campaign Against Racial Discrimination) was abandoned, and white liberals were kept at bay to avoid the experiences of the UCPA.

The Racial Adjustment Society as this organisation was so named, otherwise known as RAAS, very quickly became an effective vehicle for organising black people. Roy became National Organiser, travelled extensively to various parts of Britain and became well known in the whole of Britain. RAAS had its own media and was slowly becoming a force with which the media and the establishment had to contend.

"Brothers and sisters" said a RAAS newsletter at the time, "you've got to learn how to deal with this white man. You used to turn your cheek when he hit you...stop turning...hit him back". The initials RAAS simultaneously make up the Westindian word for a sanitary towel, an obscenity, and an African word for "leader". Such symbolism was appropriate to a movement which was to blend mysticism with militancy.

RAAS was important in its support of the 900 striking black textile workers at Courtaulds Factory in Preston in the summer of 1965. It was the first strike of black workers in Britain. RAAS members in the area called for help. Roy, Malik and Patel went down. Although they had no experience in trade union work, they sued Courtaulds on behalf of the workers. This catapulted RAAS, Roy and Malik into public prominence.

With this prominence came the inevitable internal squabbles, centred around the personalities of Roy, Malik, Jan Carew and Abdullah Patel. It was an organisation which was too top heavy, with too many leaders, all with their own idiosyncracies, their own ambitions.

Malik was a black Muslim and a disciple of the American black Muslim leader Elijah Mohammed, who had a great influence on Malik. "I knew", Roy says, "when I joined RAAS that Michael was a Muslim. I was prepared to work with Muslim and non-Muslim, Christian and non-Christian, solely to bring about a black movement. Then as time went on I realised that Michael was a Muslim first and instead of concentrating more on the political issues involving black people, he was concentrating on the religious aspect." This, Roy argues, was not good for RAAS, as there were black people from different religions or no religion at all, and instead of uniting black people, it was driving them apart. The Islamic mysticism exuded by Malik rather impeded any development of a genuine black movement. This also worried Jan Carew who was less given to the semi-religious rhetoric that Malik used. Carew's political attitudes were informed by a rigorous logic and he saw writing as part of the political battle. "At this stage, Africa should be producing her own pre-revolutionary Gorky", he said, although he was too modest to see himself as any fulfilment of this analogy.

"I found myself and Malik drifting apart. I believed from my little experience that if you cannot get on with people in an organisation there are two things you can do – stay in the organisation and be ineffective or stay in and fight. I decided I could not stay in and fight, neither did I want to stay in and be ineffective. I left", Roy says. He was frustrated by the whole experience as he had gathered around him many people who were looking to him for leadership which he could not give. "The only reason people looked towards me for leadership was maybe because there was a certain charisma or charm, or maybe an ability on my part to articulate the black man's problem. I was indeed more interested in articulating the black man's problem. I was more interested articulating the black man's problem as a catalyst rather than as a leader." Although he refused publicly to attack Malik and other black leaders, his experience in RAAS has left him very sour about other black leaders. On the other hand his formation of various black organisations and subsequent desertion of them has resulted in criticism being levelled at him that he wants to be a leader of black people. Some have gone so far as to accuse him of mere opportunism. To this he simply replies that, "history will judge me."

His continued oratory at Hyde Park brought him into conflict with the police. On one occasion, whilst speaking on the subject of rights of black people to settle in Britain he was harangued by a white woman whilst quoting irrefutable historical scholarship. She was so incensed by the logic of his argument that she resorted to violence. Roy was arguing that Britain was not a racially homogeneous society but was composed of a succession of immigrant groups. The Vikings and Romans in ancient times, the Irish, the Welsh, the Scottish, the Huguenots and the Jews in recent times. Black settlement was part of this historical continuity of migration. "Although she was Welsh, she preferred to see herself as passionately English. In the exchanges of viewpoints, she insisted that she was British and he was not. Roy, seeing the futility of further logic, brought the altercation to an end by an ironic concession. "Maybe you are right in your insistence on your exclusive nationality, but given your ignorance, you are a British *object* rather than a British subject." At this point she stormed to his soap box, hit him with her umbrella and attempted to slap his face. Roy retaliated immediately, and returned the blow. A policeman, ever watchful for breaches of the peace, arrested him even though the policeman saw the whole incident and knew that Roy was merely defending himself. Although Lord Gifford, a sympathetic advocate, argued Roy's case in the Magistrate's Court, he was still found guilty and fined £10. This was the first of a series of oppressive engagements with the police at Hyde Park.

On another occasion, when descended upon by a mob of young National Front supporters, Roy, with the support of some black people in the audience, fought off the attack, and in the process bruised the forehead of one of the thugs. For this he was instantly arrested and frogmarched through the park to the local station, and charged. Subsequent to this incident, the police would deliberately attend Roy's Sunday addresses, and would be seen taking notes. As he stepped off the podium, he would frequently be cautioned that he would be reported to the Director of Public Prosecutions for inciting racial violence. A comic example of police oversensitivity to his presence, and to the increasingly large numbers of people he attracted, took place when he once replied to a question from the audience as to his, "effectiveness as a black speaker". Roy, with typical flamboyance and Caribbean wit, announced, "When I was in Moscow, the subsequent assassin of President Kennedy was one of the people who attended one of my public speeches in Red Square. And only last week, the man who stabbed the South African ambassador, was standing here listening to me." The crowd exploded with laughter but the humour escaped the police. The following Sunday, as he approached Hyde Park, he was swiftly picked up by five plain clothes policemen, bundled into a van and taken to West End Police Station to be questioned for five hours. "I kept laughing and telling them that it was only a joke in the tradition of Hyde Park oratory, but they were serious and stone faced". He was eventually released after having managed to persuade them of his innocence.

Between 1965 and 1968, Roy was arrested on at least fifteen occasions in Hyde Park, the much vaunted location of British freedom of speech and expression. His "crimes" were various: obstruction of the police, refusal to leave the Park when ordered to do so, causing affray, all of which were unnecessary and undeserved charges. Roy says, "such police action is a good example of the criminalisation of the black community."

Protection under the 1968 Race Relations Act. Roy Sawh is being cautioned that anything he may say may be taken down and used against him

Chapter Five

In 1965, the Race Relations Act, which was allegedly aimed at outlawing racial discrimination and activities which could lead to racial unrest, was passed. "The next thing I knew, the police came to Hyde Park and told me they were cautioning me and would report me to the Director of Public Prosecutions as I was contravening Section 6-1B of the Race Relations Act. I did not know how I could be contravening this Act as I had been speaking in Hyde Park for a number of years by then. I was cautioned a few more times and was eventually arrested and charged under the Act. I then realised the witch hunt was on.

Roy explains what it is that he said on that occasion: "One of the audience asked me how I would solve racial injustice if I was in South Africa. I replied in a jocular fashion that in South Africa, every white family has a black cook, and that I would ensure that every black cook would have half-an-ounce of rat poison." Upon a subsequent question as to how he would solve the British problem: "The British claim to hate Indians because of the smell of curry and garlic, yet, when you go to Indian restaurants they are packed with white people. I would have to tell the Chef to put something hot in the curry." He drew the audience's attention to the invaluable and unrewarded contribution of black doctors in the British National Health Service. "You know that over 40% of British doctors are black, and if you get me angry, I will have to tell them to give you the right injections at the wrong time." For these consciously humourous and harmless pronouncements, Roy was tried under the Race Relations Act.

Roy was tried under the Act and was fined £120 (or eight months in jail) – ironically one of the first victims of legislation instigated by white liberals whose target had been white discrimination. "I well remember the moment of arrest. At five in the morning Commander Newman, who was until recently the Metropolitan Police Commissioner, and a group of officers, came to my flat with a warrant of arrest and served me with a *deportation order* which however, they were not able to carry out. The whole episode was a bizarre testimony of white officialdom. I refused to pay the fine on principle and was sentenced to eight months imprisonment. I spent two miserable and defiant weeks in Brixton prison, and was released when a Swedish friend of mine, Alf Lundin, read about the case in *The Times* in Sweden and he paid the fine."

He is reticent when pressed to talk about his prison experience. "I can only say that prisons are not made for human beings. I wouldn't want even a dog to be locked up there for one night."

The trial and fine made Roy a hero of the black community, as it did Malik, who also fell foul of the Race Relations Act. But it also completely shattered all illusions he might have had of British justice. "By the end of my trial I did not believe any more in the British system or in British fair play. All I was asking for was for black people to have a fair deal in Britain, but instead of getting praise, I was convicted."

His experiences with the police made him realise the difficulties black people encountered once they came into conflict with the law. "As a result I found myself going to the police station to stand bail for people, visiting tribunals, representing black people when they had problems with landlords, and slowly I found myself doing a sort of social work which became part of my duty because I was involved."

He established contact with lawyers and solicitors, housing associations and other voluntary organisations. This he did voluntarily. Some of his friends recognised what he was doing and decided to pay his rent every week, with a small amount for pocket money. This went on for about seven months. As the work increased, his shortcomings became obvious. "I was not a trained social worker, and frequently I did not know what to do when a serious problem arose. I felt I had to have a little more formal learning in sociology." So after further soul-searching, he went to Fircroft College at Birmingham to study sociology. "I was very pleased to be in a place where knowledge was being disseminated. I felt there was a lot I could learn. I had a problem getting a grant but overcame that, thanks to various friends."

But the usual problems arose. "I could not sit there and listen to my professor without questioning him. The study of sociology was not related to the reality of the suffering of black people as I knew it. When we did economic history he treated

From Where I Stand 43

black history as being irrelevant or unimportant. And that part of black history which is related to the British empire was completely left out. Naturally I developed an open hostility to my lecturers and professor and gradually refused to take part in any educational training which seemed to have no relevance to the problems of black people."

Roy became very active in student politics and was elected President of the Student's Union during the first month he was at college. He started to amend the rules and regulations governing the committee. This brought him into direct conflict with the resident principal and petty arguments ensued.

He used to visit the Handsworth area of Birmingham, and other cities in the Midlands, where he addressed black workers. "A lot of black people knew I was in Birmingham and so whenever a problem arose – like a dispute with landlords or a strike – they would come to the campus, ask my opinion and take me back to their area to talk to people. I found myself spending a lot of time in the black community whereas I should have been studying."

While he was there he organised a successful Black Power Youth Conference where black leaders like Tariq Ali came to speak. "I was still at the college and at one stage found it impossible as I could not get on with the lecturers. When I asked questions about racism and the anti-black attitude of the white working class, no answers were forthcoming. I found myself in an institution which consisted primarily of people who were pro-establishment. All they were prepared to do was get hold of the dissidents among the working class movement, bring them to these colleges, socialise them and hope that they would go out as social reformers rather than potential revolutionaries."

Frustration was so great that in June after the Easter recess he was seriously asking himself what he was at. Should he continue, should he return to London and maybe form another black organisation, or join one? "I just could not bring myself around to really see the role I could play in relation to black people in this country". He used to come to London every Sunday to speak at Hyde Park. "Then one day going back on the train the idea suddenly hit me. It went something like this: If you are at a college of the establishment and they are not teaching you what you would like to be taught, and since you do not expect society to do so, what then prevents you from creating an institution which would fulfil this need? Back at college I sat up all night and thought about the idea. It had to be free. Black people in Britain are at the bottom of the economic ladder. The courses must therefore be given free of charge to all who wish to take part. I returned to London and discussed the idea with some friends."

At university he refused to participate in studies. "I was a rebel now", he says. He started to put ideas about the Free University on paper. It would be anti-establishment, anti-institutional and had to be a place of learning. "So Free University. Free University for what? Afro-Asian studies, Third World studies? As I was a leading advocate of Black Power and in my definition and that of many of my friends "black" as a political definition included the Third World, Black Studies was the obvious name. So, the Free University of Black Studies. I discussed it with my friends, convinced them, not of success but at least of the potential of success. The Management Committee of Toc H, a charitable organisation, made a room available to us at 24 Pembridge Gardens, Notting Hill. We distributed leaflets at Hyde Park Corner and to our amazement about 130 people turned up." And that is how the Free University, which can be regarded as an educational experiment of a unique character within this country, came about.

"Many white and black people have wanted to know why it was essential to have a Black Studies centre in Britain. I can only answer by saying that it is important for us to understand why there are black people in this country and elsewhere in the 'developed' world. European colonial policies have, over a period of years, resulted in people being actively drawn to the West for education and livelihood. Any group coming to this country will want to find its own identity if there is to be a genuine multi-racial society in Britain. Integration, where there is absorption of one culture by another, assumes that the existing society is best; this can be no solution. In addition, there are an increasing number of British citizens who were born in this country but whose parents were black. Many of these people are suffering traumatic crises of identity and I feel that a black centre is part of a solution to this problem. Black studies in Britain can help to provide the necessary backgrounds to enable groups to be aware of their own history and culture and to take their full place in a pluralistic society.

"The history of black people has long been one of oppression. Once other oppressed people have found identification with black people and their problems and so black studies has come to mean the study of history and the present situation of

From Where I Stand

THE FREE UNIVERSITY FOR BLACK STUDIES
Achin Preminder

Westindian Digest June/July, 1973

In Summer 1968 in a small flat in Notting Hill Gate, two West Indians, Roy Sawh from Guyana and Stephen Bulgin from Jamaica, rapping together about the black scene in Britain and about the world scene in general, discovered and unfolded among themselves the concept of a "Free University for Black Studies" in Britain. Its meaning and purpose was declared in the title itself.

By "black" were meant all

Roy Sawh

all exploited peoples. It is important to realise that history has for too long been viewed from the standpoint of the whites and that a valid contribution to academic thought can be made by studying history from the point of view of the blacks and by striving to correct the distortion of history as presented by the white colonial classes. My experience at Fircroft College confirmed this viewpoint."

A growing library, stocked with works on black history, books by black authors, and black periodical magazines from all parts of the world has been set up, and people lecturing in the Free University had come from a variety of backgrounds, from militant trade unionists and African freedom fighters to authors, churchmen and university lecturers. They had all given their service free. The University met on four evenings a week. On Monday evenings, African affairs were discussed, on Wednesday, Asian affairs and on Friday, Latin American and Caribbean affairs and a study of Marxist-Leninism. Thursdays had been given to subjects like mathematics and physics. In general terms, they had been, according to Roy and others, very encouraged by the growing numbers of people, both black and white, who regularly came to the Free University and they were now assured of a gathering of 40-50 on any one night. Students did not need entrance qualifications, nor did they study for examinations, or pay for their tuition. It was organised by its members, thus creating an atmosphere for informed dialogue which educated the members of this university in a way that, in other places, would have been restricted by the conventional student-teacher relationship. Because of this independent nature of the Free University, it pursued studies from the standpoint of its individual members without the constraints implicit in a degree awarding system. The teaching atmosphere was relaxed and discussion flowed freely. To certain academicians this might have appeared to be anarchic but in the eyes of the students it was essential as it did not reinforce the dominative situation which results when the relationship between teacher and student is an authoritative one. Over £2,000 had been raised towards a permanent building – £1,000 having been donated by the World Council of Churches. Roy's dominance in the centre cannot be denied. There is no doubt that the name Free University of Black Studies was synonymous with that of Roy Sawh, Black Power leader in Britain.

An inquiry among members of the Free University revealed that they believed that the level of black consciousness had to be raised, and the solidarity of black people expressed. This, Roy agrees, was a commitment to the idea of Black Power in the sense of black people having more say over the decisions which affect their own lives rather than a necessary alignment with the "Black Power Movement" and its widely publicised activities. "The idea of Black Power", he says, "is indeed relevant to any society where there are oppressed and exploited people". It was this militancy which made the classes black in audience and discouraged orthodox liberal academicians from supporting the University materially and otherwise. As Roy Sawh said at the time. "We are now moving into the stage at the Free University of a careful political analysis of the black presence in Britain and are trying to relate it to what is happening in Africa and Asia, not only from a cultural point of view, because we don't believe that when every black person has had a dashiki and an Afro hair cut our problems will be solved. It is rather the economic and geographic location of one's country which determines its state of development. All this can only be done by knowing who you are, where you are and where you are going. This is what the Free University intends to do after the two years it has been in existence".

In 1974 *The Westindian World,* which was then Britain's only black newspaper, was in financial trouble and a donation of £2,000 was given to the newspaper from the Free University for Black Studies.

This was one small example of the way the University contributed to the needs of the black community. The work of the University assisted in campaigning for "black studies" to be introduced into the British Educational curriculum. Bodies like the Inner London Education Authority (ILEA) began, in a small, haphazard way to recognise the need and encouraged schools to re-examine their syllabuses and teaching practices. Severe strain on the University's resources eventually led in 1974 to the disbanding of the organisation, with its members moving back to their local areas to share their ideas with their communities.

Many of them made an input into the development of supplementary schools which were seen as a stop-gap, emergency measure to encounter the failings of the white establishment schools.

Chapter Six

Looking back over the whole venture Roy explained how white liberals played an important role at the inception of the Free University for Black Studies, but had subsequently slowly withdrawn their involvement and support. Part of the blame for the demise of the UCPA was also placed at the doorstep of white liberals.

"I think in the early days of our struggle a lot of black people had a lot of hope and confidence in white liberals. They were glad to meet whites who were not racist, who were not openly hostile to them and who were prepared to listen and do something. I think at one stage of our development we genuinely believed that white liberals were our friends.

"But as time progressed, we found that white liberals wanted to control us. They wanted to tell us what to do and how to do our thing. They lionised us. As a result we listened more to them than to our own people. And as a result we lost contact with our people.

"As we realised what they were up to, and became more articulate and independent, they felt they were being cut off. Well they were cut off because their attitudes was often patronising, condescending – 'never mind, everything is going to be all right, I am here to help you', is how they felt. They wanted their own solution and would have tied us to a system we did not want to be part of anyway."

In April, 1969, prior to the formation of the Free University for Black Studies and after he had parted with Michael X, Roy together with Jagmohan Joshi, Birmingham leader of the Indian Workers' Association, had successfully established the Black Peoples Alliance (BPA), which had about fifty organisations affiliated to it by 1970.

The BPA which organised the Rhodesian demonstration that ended with the attack on South Africa House in January, 1969, was perhaps the nearest thing to a national Black Power body, although essentially its strength derived from Joshi's Birmingham following.

This mosaic of "groupmuscles" was deceptive, however. "We were all very temperamental people", says Roy. "we fought and argued like hell, but this fighting and arguing was where we got most of our thinking done. We tolerated each other immensely". But how much? The events surrounding his call early in 1969 for a May Day strike by black workers were typical of the weaknesses that afflict black organisations here. Roy made the call on his own initiative, and was promptly disowned by the Black Peoples' Alliance, which he had helped to establish only a year before. "It was the result of internal jealousies", he says. "Roy wanted to do things all by himself", a BPA militant claimed at the time. As a result Roy drifted away from the BPA although he never denounced or acted against them.

After this experience, he spent most of his time organising the Free University for Black Studies, and put so much work and effort into it that other black leaders were quite surprised. "Roy was drifting no more. It seems he had finally reached a point of political stability", one said. "This is what I wanted all the time", he said. "A base from which ideas for action could grow. It was a battle ground for the mind and soul. From here cadres for the black revolution which I saw coming soon were being nurtured".

"I saw the next ten years as being crucial as far as black people were concerned in this country. I could envisage black people physically deported from this country. They would primarily be the older immigrants, and statisticians would argue that they were old and could not contribute any more towards things here. By that time they would have children in their early twenties. With conditions as they were – bad educational facilities, high unemployment – these youngsters would not have learned any skilled trades, nor would they be literate. With this society moving into the technological age in terms of heavy industry and computerisation, a lot of black youth would find themselves doing manual jobs. There would be frustration – there were signs already – and unlike their parents they would not sit back and wait for somebody to come and change things. The result appeared obvious. Others would turn to petty crime, for example involving drugs, which were becoming a real problem amongst youths. This was the biggest problem, because black people and drugs were slowly becoming synonomous. Things were getting worse daily – black kids on the street corners, no social facilities, clashes with the police and the establishment as a whole. They were already considering themselves outsiders in our society, the generation gap between their parents and themselves was widening. The establishment through the police and the various laws which hit at black people was further alienating them. Putting all this together, it was clear to me at the time that the black youth would in ten years hence become the real danger. The apathy which earlier manifested itself in sulleness and so called laziness would become the anger of tomorrow. And that anger would be channelled into a very destructive role. I saw that in ten years time we would have the same situation as in the United States repeating itself here. Yes, even I was afraid because I knew what was bottled up inside those frustrated youths. I hoped that the Free University could in some way help to channel that anger to something constructive, but I was not sure."

Chapter Seven

Although Roy Sawh is strongly influenced by Marxism, he is not purely a Marxist. "I need a two-pronged ideology", he says, "one to understand the economics of racism and one to understand the economics of class". But is there not a conflict somewhere in this strategy?

"I don't see any conflict. As a Marxist I recognise that there are members of the white working class who are oppressed. But I also realise that the majority of the white working class discriminate against me, rightly or wrongly, because I am black. I accept the class analysis as a Marxist and I accept that when the economic structure changes then these problems will disappear. But I am not the type of Marxist who will sit back and wait for the super-economic structure to change before my problems as a black person change. I know that they are against me, not because I am an accountant but because I am black. The people who are against me, against blacks, are not the white elite, because we never really meet them. It is not the white middle class. It is the working class, the very people with whom we are supposed to have everything in common. They see in the black artisan, the black worker, an economic threat to their jobs – a threat which the white middle class does not see.

"I cannot resolve this problem, despite the claims by other Marxists who say I have everything in common with the white working class. The only thing I can say to them is, "well don't tell me that, tell the person who discriminates against me, the white worker. Educate him, not me". I see our task first in organising black people and making them aware of their position. Then I see the possibilities of further politicising in line with Marxist class analysis".

He denies that this thesis leads to a polarisation of force – on the one side black and on the other white – which will inevitably lead to a racial battle. "When black people stand on their own as decent human beings in this country, white people will respect them. As long as black people have no confidence in themselves, as long as they are weak, they will be scapegoats for oppression. Once they are strong and well organised they will be respected and racism will be eased".

Did this imply that until black people were organised they had to stay aloof from issues which, as part of the community at large, concerned them as much as white people – issues such as community action and participation in the electoral process? Why has there been little attempt to play conventional political games? "I am not sure that I welcome community work where the emphasis is purely on community work. If it leads towards a political realisation of our problem then it is alright. But I am afraid that it becomes a safety valve for the system and deters black people from action."

At one time Roy announced his intention to stand in the South Kensington by-election, but withdrew before nomination day. "I withdrew because I had no faith in the constitutional process as it relates to black people". Some black people point to this action of his as another sign of his opportunism. "Roy was prepared to play the white man's game a few years ago", one black leader said. "He only withdrew because black people looked with real opprobrium on any participation".

"There are black people", Roy says, "who feel part of British society. They like the system and sometimes don't understand its mechanism. They think a few reforms will alter the system and make things better for them. I don't go for this idea completely, but I do agree that there are certain instances where the constitutional machinery can be used to help certain sections of the black community. This unfortunately tends to create the situation where those black people then think that the system is good".

Where black people are a substantial number in a community and where it is possible for them to put up candidates, they should. In this way they can represent the interests of black people as far as housing, rents etc., are concerned. But I would not concentrate all energies towards this kind of activity. Also, putting up black candidates and not getting them elected, or getting them elected and exposing their limitations, helps in the further disillusionment of the electoral processes and the four established British political parties. Although I want no part of capitalism or racism and my aim still remains to destroy the source of racism, for those who still feel that there is something left in this society which is redeemable, then there is the ballot box. I am prepared to go along with this view, but I am convinced we are taking part in a masochistic exercise".

Chapter Eight

In early 1971, thirteen years after he had boarded, penniless, that third class Italian boat to Southampton, a nattily dressed Roy Sawh disembarked from the Prince of Netherlands boat at Georgetown, Guyana. There was a crowd to meet him this time. The Georgetown papers had announced his arrival. One headline read "Roy Sawh, Guyanese leader in Britain, returns home on visit", with a two column picture of him and a ten inch write up.

It was a satisfying recognition, he surmised; he had been looking forward to this trip for years, and was keen to see the progress that had been made in his country during his absence. He was impressed with the new airport which he later visited, although he could not remember how the old one looked as he had not seen it when he was in Georgetown thirteen years ago. He also visited other Westindian territories and was disgusted by what he saw. He said, "I was full of expectations – great ones at that. I came back sympathetic and hopeful, but left disappointed. The poor had got poorer and the rich richer. More Westindian countries had become more corrupt. Independence was only a facade. So much so that any politician who genuinely believed in social justice would not even attempt to use the parliamentary machine."

Did he then advocate a violent overthrow of the existing governments as the only way out? In one of his speeches at that time he addressed himself to this question:

"Today in the Westindies we have black leaders who have taken political control of an economic order which is determined by western countries. They are, therefore, running a system which is exploitative, which is determined to exploit the majority of the people in order that a few can be the beneficiaries. Comparably, the corruption which took place under Batista in Cuba is there in the Westindies today. It is a similar situation to the one before Castro took over. When socialism comes to the Westindies it will go through a transitional stage. It will take time and in that process there will be counter-revolution, and you will have foreigners intervening to safeguard their interests. There might be civil wars, killings might take place. But this should not deter us, because if we are going to worry about people who will die, or be killed, then there will be no change in the society whatsoever. Only a Cuban type of revolution will be the answer to the problems in the Westindies."

It seems he did not see anything amiss in the aspect of dependence of Cuba on the Soviet Union or the possibility of any future socialist Caribbean country being dependent on the Soviet Union or other Eastern European countries. Neither did his earlier anti-Soviet utterances and activities prevent him from saying that, "if socialism was to come to Guyana or the Westindies, it would have to depend in its early stages on fraternal countries and on socialist countries. The question of total independence does not become an issue. What is important is to establish contacts with friendly socialist countries in order to give time for change. Then you might see some kind of independence".

Fighting words, but how was he going to put them into operation? This he did not seem to have worked out. "The black people returning from Britain to the Westindies are so quickly and so easily bought over by good government jobs that you cannot look to many of them for support, for any sustained movement way back home. That is one of the difficult jobs we have here in Britain. Many come to this country penniless and with little education. Those who go back, return better educated, better off financially. The burden of any change lies with us who remain here. It is our job to bring change here and in that way help to weaken one of the external supports which prop up unpopular governments way back home."

Upon termination of his holidays in Guyana he flew back to England via the Westindian islands, but his reputation as a Black Power activist had preceded him. A Black Power conference was being planned in Bermuda, with talk of setting up Black Power cells all over the Caribbean. He was harrassed by immigration officials at Trinidad's Airport and allowed only 24 hours stopover. He flew on to Grenada to see Maurice Bishop whom he had known in London, but after five days sojourn there, an Inspector of Police came to his hotel, declared that he was *personna non grata*, and escorted him to the airport. A 'plane took him to Barbados, and the Immigration

Authorities there, after an hour of interrogation, gave him enough time to catch the next 'plane out of the country, irrespective of its destination. The next flight was from Barbados to Bermuda, but on landing at the airport there, Roy was refused permission to land. Fortunately, the same 'plane flew on to London. "I had to work for the next three years paying for all those unneccessary 'plane fares", he says wryly.

Part Two

FROM WHERE I STAND is the title of a pamphlet published by Roy Sawh himself. It summarises the content of his oratory at Speaker's Corner in Hyde Park.

"FROM WHERE I STAND"

by Roy Sawh, 1980

What is the history of the immigrants, but the history of the British Empire? And what is the history of the British Empire but the history of Asia, Africa and the Caribbean? And what is the history of all these peoples, but the history of the most pitiless and cruel exploitation by white people throughout the Black world?

Do you know why the sun never sets on the British Empire? Because God did not trust an Englishman in the dark! After 200 years teaching the Indians, the English language, every Indian today speaks English like Peter Sellers! Ladies and Gentlemen, I hope that with the weather permitting, it will be possible today to have a very good meeting, and I do hope that you will be prepared to take part, so that we can learn together, and by learning together, I hope that we will be able to change the repugnant views that we hold about each other.

My meeting is a very controversial one and I hope that people will be able to understand the controversy, although I don't think there is any controversy because I am using history as my guideline. This is the most informative meeting place in Hyde Park - people come here to learn, even the police are here taking notes, so you see how important this meeting is!

Let me begin by saying that in every country in the world where English is spoken and where the Anglo-Saxon culture is practised you have racist immigration laws, and so-called racial problems. And those societies which exist today, are in countries that are Black people's. They may call these laws by different names, depending on the cultural development of their society, but in actual fact, these laws have the same effects.

In the United States of America it is called the McCarran Act. In Canada, they call it the "Anti-Asiatic White Preferential Immigration Bill" not forgetting that these countries were originally inhabited by Black people. The word 'Canada' originated from an Indian word, 'Canata'. In New Zealand, they call it "The Selected Immigration Scheme" and in Australia, they call it "The White Australian Policy". In Rhodesia, they call it "UDI". In South Africa, they call it "Apartheid", and in Britain, the mother country of them all, they call it "The Commonwealth Immigration Act".

If Jesus Christ had lived in London, the English would have called him an immigrant: probably, that is why he never came to England. By following the historical development of the past, I pray every day and night "Please God, please don't allow the English to go to heaven, because if you do I am sure that the English will introduce immigration laws to keep out the Blacks".

When you consider that most of the countries I have mentioned so far were originally Black people's countries, and the English went to these countries, without an invitation, and took complete control: I wonder if this is what they assume Black people would do in England? I have got news for the English people - no Black man or Black woman in his or her right senses would like to take control of England, because the English are so stupid and lazy that there is no way anyone can help! Even a Roman Governor, Cicero, residing in London wrote a letter to his counterpart, Atticus in Rome saying that the "English were so lazy that they will never make good slaves". I know that there are many of you who will say that I have no reason for saying that the English are stupid, but let me tell you that I have got many, many reasons for saying so. Take a good look in London: go down to Queensway where you will find Bayswater Station and then go down to Bayswater where you will find Queensway Station.

The English will always ask, why did we come to England? But ladies and gentlemen, the mere idea that an English person asks a question like that makes one realise immediately that the person does not know very much about his or her history. How can an English person ask such a stupid question? When at the same time the historians write about how the white man discovered us. All Black people in England today came from what is and what was the British Empire. We are the Empire.

According to the white man, he came to civilise and educate us, that we are British subjects and Britain is our Mother Country, and anytime we wanted to come "home" we should come: now that we have come, Mummy doesn't like it! The white man gave us British passports to travel with. We were not asked whether we wanted to be British, we were not consulted before the white man imposed his cultural values and language upon us. We were told "you are British" and now the white man has changed his mind and is saying "No, you are not British, you are all immigrants". It is very funny, when the white man arrived in our country he called himself a Settler, and when Black people arrived in the white man's country, he called us Immigrants. That is why I believe that we are living in a world, where white is right and Black is wrong. If a white man is to do anything, he must be right because he is white, but if a Black man is to do the same thing, he could be wrong because he is Black! Take the case of Andy Young: he was dismissed for talking with the PLO, but in order for President Carter to get help in releasing the hostages in Iran, he, President Carter, is talking to the PLO. Who would dismiss President Carter?

For too long the white man has oppressed us in our own countries and in his. The time has come when we are saying enough is enough. He will have to take note and change or he will plunge the world into a racial war. The next world war will not be based on the contradiction between the East and West, but on the arrogance of the white man against the Black man. The Black people are fed up and have had enough of the White man; either the white man has to change or we will have to change him. Making all these points in public, many of you will call me a racist, but ladies and gentlemen, there is no such thing as a Black racist - what you have heard is anger coming from a Black man.

When you were threatened by Hitler, you did not negotiate, you did something positive to stop it, otherwise you would be speaking German today like we speak English and then the German people will tell you 200 years later how they educated and civilised you, the same way you are telling the Blacks of today. It's an irony that when white people are fighting against oppression from other people, they tend to glorify their actions, but when Black people are fighting against oppression, whites condemn Black resistance to their oppression by using emotive phrases, i.e. 'Terrorists' and 'Guerillas'.

The arguments for colonising Black people have been used by white historians in order to justify the rape and pillage of our countries. It is always the white historians who have been writing about how inferior the Black races are. From the days of "Long", the white scientists are still searching for the gene that would prove the inferiority of the Black races. Never in the writings of Black writers has anyone ever suggested or even attempted to prove that the whites are inferior. Psychologists will agree with me, that people who are inferior will try to prove that they are superior in order to hide their inferiority.

All our history has been written by white people. They even went so far as to say that Colombus discovered America, not that Colombus was the first white man to arrive in America. The mere idea that you are saying that you discovered America is implying that nothing was there, and by the stroke of a pen you have written off hundreds of years of civilisation of the Aztecs and the Incas. This is intellectual dishonesty. They went on to say that "Clive" discovered India. What a joke! Then, Lawrence of Arabia discovered the Arabs! Marco Polo discovered China and Livingstone discovered Africa. You see ladies and gentlemen, we were all asleep and this white man came and said to us: "You are discovered", and we jumped up with such great delight, that two million of us ended up in Britain. I hope that when we write white people's history, we will not be as arrogant as the white historians. Can you imagine the whites in South Africa saying that they were in Africa before the African? What would white people say if Black people were to say that they were in Brixton before the whites? During the Second World War there were many Black men in British uniforms fighting against the Germans for Britain, and when they make a film about the war, they never show you a Black soldier. Who are the racists? They used to tell Black people that if Hitler had won the war, Blacks would have to do the dirty jobs! When the Americans make a film about the wars between the Indians and the whites, every time the white man wins the war.

It's called good planning, and when the Indians win a war, the white man calls it an 'ambush'. We are good to come and run the buses and the trains: our women folk in the hospitals

Members of Flight 16 at Filey Camp, Yorkshire, March, 1944

and old people's homes, caring, cleaning and cooking for the whites, but when it comes to equal opportunities, the white man has to introduce the 'Race Relations Act'. To legislate against racism in this country is as effective as legislating against syphilis. The Race Relations Act was introduced to protect Black people and up to the time of writing, more Black people have been prosecuted and convicted than white people, at last, the white man is beginning to realise that the days for "gunboat diplomacy" are over and unless he can come to terms with the idea that all men are created equal in the eyes of God, he will persist and continue to discriminate against us. We shall rise up, using whatever means are necessary to free ourselves from his oppression. Black and white people can co-exist as long as the white man is prepared to judge us by our own standards and not his, because his are not just. To each according to his own. Integration is a subterfuge for retaining white supremacy.

The attitude of the police to Blacks is of great concern to us, and if this white society continues to ignore the 'cries' of the Blacks regarding police brutality and 'SUS', then the relationship between the police and the Black Community will worsen. When this happens, the repercussions will be international and the majority will always win. We are the majority in the world. We will win the struggle for human dignity. All men are born free, but are enslaved by others. Slavery has been abolished since 1833, but slavery continues by other names, i.e. immigrants, guest workers, etc. A slave ceases to be a slave only when he can redefine the definitions imposed upon him, and when we write history we will not write about the Second World War, but the Second European Tribal War - after all, the war was fought mostly among white nations. The white man has never stopped talking about humanity, yet he has never ceased in his search to destroy it. When white people talk about human rights, they don't mean Black people in South Africa; they mean white dissidents in the Eastern countries. The white man even claims that he was "invited" to Vietnam to stop Communism, and he killed and killed; but when the Cubans were invited to Angola to fight against colonialism and oppression this action was contrary to the Western interest. Even the Pope did not condemn what Hitler was doing in Europe because Hitler threatened to bomb his summer palace!

Unfortunately, we live in a world where white is right and right is might and might means power and all the power is in the hands of the whites and yet they talk of equality of peoples.

What a farce!

So the Soviets are in Afghanistan, and the West is worried. I wonder if the East was worried when the Americans were in Vietnam? The same argument that the Americans were using to justify their presence in Vietnam, are the same arguments the Soviets are using for being in Afghanistan. The Soviets are accused of being expansionist, but the Americans and the British were doing the same, but they call that the Organisation of American States and the British Empire. Since when are the Americans and the British concerned about the welfare of Islamic tribesmen living in the mountains and about Pakistanis to the extent that they are prepared to give them arms to defend themselves against the Soviets, but when Indians and Pakistanis arrive in Britain, they are subjected to degrading treatment by the British Immigration Officers; they even carry out virginity tests on Asian women.

The Soviets are doing exactly what the British have done, and what the Americans are doing. The truth of the matter is that the Soviets have caught the Americans with their trousers down, and they are naked in the eyes of the world.

Before they consider economic sanctions against Iran, how about trying it against South Africa. In Iran there are 49 white hostages: in South Africa, there are 17 million Black hostages. Where is justice most needed?

It does not matter by what names we called them, when I say Black and White, you know about whom I am talking. When I talk about Black Power, many white people become very hysterical, but because of the geo-political divisions of the world today, you don't have to talk about White Power, but you call it NATO and the EEC and when Black Nations are trying to get together, you call it "Third World": where are the First and Second Worlds, I wonder? Many people object and call me a racist because I talk about Black and White people but ladies and gentlemen, does it matter whether you call them people from the developing world, people from the Southern world, people from the Primary Producing Countries or people from the under-industrialised Nations? Does it really matter, when in actual fact, we are talking about two kinds of people - white people against black people?

Let me give you a classic example: when the Africans were fighting for their land in Kenya against the whites, the Africans were called Mau-Mau. When the Vietnamese were fighting for their land against the Americans, they were called Viet Cong.

When the Palestinians are fighting for their land against the Zionists they are called Terrorists. When the Blacks in Rhodesia were fighting for their land against the Whites, they were called Guerillas: but when the French were fighting against the Germans for their land, they were called Resistance Fighters and when the Hungarians were fighting for their land against the Soviets, they were called "Freedom Fighters". Every revolution in the world is based on the question of land. But the white man would like the Black people's revolution to be based on "Integration" and "Multi-racialism", rather than being based on Land, because the white man realises that if the Black man's revolution was based on land the white man will be dispossessed. The emergence of Black independent nations is only the beginning for the control of the Black people's natural resources for the benefit of Black people. There will be many organisations like OPEC (Organisation of Petroleum Exporting Countries) being formed in the Black world.

We have seen what effects OPEC has had on the Western economy, and I doubt if the Western World would ever allow organisations like OPEC to be formed in the Black world again. That brings me to another matter - the question of nuclear weapons. Most of the nuclear weapons in this world are in the possession of white nations (if or because of a misunderstanding between any two white nations, the whole world would suffer). Black people are more than two thirds of the world's population: why should Black people suffer because of the disagreement between two white nations? If the argument for more nuclear weapons is based on the principles of self-defence, then why shouldn't Black nations possess nuclear weapons too. I remember when India exploded the first bomb, there was a big cry in the Western papers and when Pakistan was in the process of trying to make one, Western journalists and photographers went to take pictures which violated the national security of Pakistan. When nuclear fall-out was discovered in Southern Africa, the West did not even mention any condemnation of South Africa. I will argue that if Western nations have the right to possess nuclear weapons, then any Black nation should also have the right to possess them. After all we are the majority in the world, and if Democracy is for the people, by the people, and with the people, then let Black people have a say in whether they live or die. Going back into the past, I don't think any Black leaders will ever trust white leaders when it comes to the welfare of Black people. How come white people have changed when not so long ago they were killing black people in their own countries? Historically, I know that Black people have killed Black people; white people have also killed white people. White people have left their countries and gone to Black people's countries and killed them, but I don't know when Black people have left their countries and killed white people. That is the difference which I am talking about.

Even when the Moors ruled Spain for 700 years, they did not impose their religion on the Spanish people, as a matter of fact, they – the Moors – built the first University in the World for Secular Learning: The University of Kardovah – that is still there for everyone to see. Tell me, where in any British colony did the white man not impose his religion, language and cultural values on the Black people? The white man claims that he came to Africa and India to civilise us, but ladies and gentlemen, when the first white man arrived in Benin in 1490 on the West Coast of Africa, they saw a sewerage system in existence, when in the same period where in Europe did you have a sewerage system? When the white man arrived in India there was a culture and civilisation in existence. There were industries and an organised society: the palaces and historical buildings were already built.

The Taj Mahal was built by Indians, one of the wonders of the world. Can an uncivilised people build the Taj Mahal? An Indian who loved his wife very much wanted to show the world his love for a woman. Whenever you go to India and you look at the Taj Mahal, you will see an Indian erection for the love of a woman.

The white man did not colonise Iceland or Greenland because there were no raw materials and cheap labour available: so when the white man tells us that he came to educate and civilise us, he is being dishonest and very arrogant. If it was true that he came to educate us, and it only takes 21 years to educate a child and the white man was in our countries for more than 200 years, how come that Black people are still illiterate and uneducated according to the white man? The white man is greedy and he came to our countries because of what we had to offer - cheap supply of raw materials, and a guaranteed market to sell his manufactured goods. The reason was economics and not because we were heathens and he wanted to Christianise us. First and foremost, the white man is not a Christian. He may use Christianity when it suits him, and the guns when it doesn't. In England, on Sundays, most of the churches are empty and most of the pubs are full! This is commercial Christianity. Jesus Christ was born in Palestine. In that period of time, most people in that area were Black, yet when you go to a white man's church you see Jesus Christ's statue in white, with blond hair, ginger beard and blue eyes. Jesus Christ was not a white man, he was a Black man. The White man goes to church and prays to a Black man whom he calls Jesus Christ and goes home to have a cup of tea: most of the things he consumes at the table comes from Black people's countries, and when he goes on the streets and sees a Black man he shouts: "Why don't you niggers go home?" Every year at Christmas time all his Santa Claus' are white, even when he comes down the chimney he is still white!

Kwame Ture (formerly Stokely Carmichael) and Roy Sawh, 1985

Released from prison, 1981

ROY SAWH FREED

Narayan Masterminded The Defence

ROY SAWH, the popular Hyde Park orator who was jailed by an Old Bailey judge three months ago on an 'incitement' charge, was released from Wormwood Scrubs prison last Monday, following a successful appeal hearing at the High Court of Justice in the Strand.

The appeal, which was masterminded by Britain's leading black barrister, Mr Rudy Narayan, was a welcome triumph for a small group of loyal friends of Mr Roy Sawh, who had formed a 'Defence Committee' following his conviction and imprisonment on May 2 of this year.

Convincing Delivery

It was not, however, the brilliant legal mind of Mr Narayan, nor the perseverance of the small Defence Committee, that completely won the day for Mr Roy Sawh. "The formidable character witness", in the words of Lord Chief Justice Waller, the senior member of the three Judges who heard the appeal, played the major role in the appellant's defence causing the three judges to unanimously agree to reduce the 3-year sentence to 12 months suspended for two years.

The court however, dismissed the conviction appeal on the ground that there wasn't fresh evidence to warrant the conviction being quashed, but complimented Mr Narayan for his forceful and convincing delivery.

A happy and relieved Mr Sawh broke into a broad smile as he walked out of the Court embracing his friends and his leading Counsel, Mr Narayan.

Asked how he felt to be free after serving three months "in the nick", Mr Roy Sawh remarked: "The feeling is good, but the experience was traumatic. Being locked up in a small cell with two other people for 23 hours a day can send any sane person bonkers, especially if one has to endure that experience for five years.

Inhumane Conditions

"I am sure that the public doesn't know of the cramped inhumane conditions that prisoners are being subject to in British prisons.

"Life in prison is de-humanising and should not even be for animals. If three dogs were locked up in a small area, like that in which prisoners have to endure, I am sure that the R.S.P.C.A. (Royal Society for the Prevention of Cruelty to Animals) would immediately prosecute the authorities."

Does this mean that Mr Sawh is now willing to lend his name to a campaigning organisation on behalf of prisoners?

"I would certainly not mind being involved in any genuine organisation which campaigns for prison reform, especially when there are so many young black people in jails.

Caribbean Times, 1981

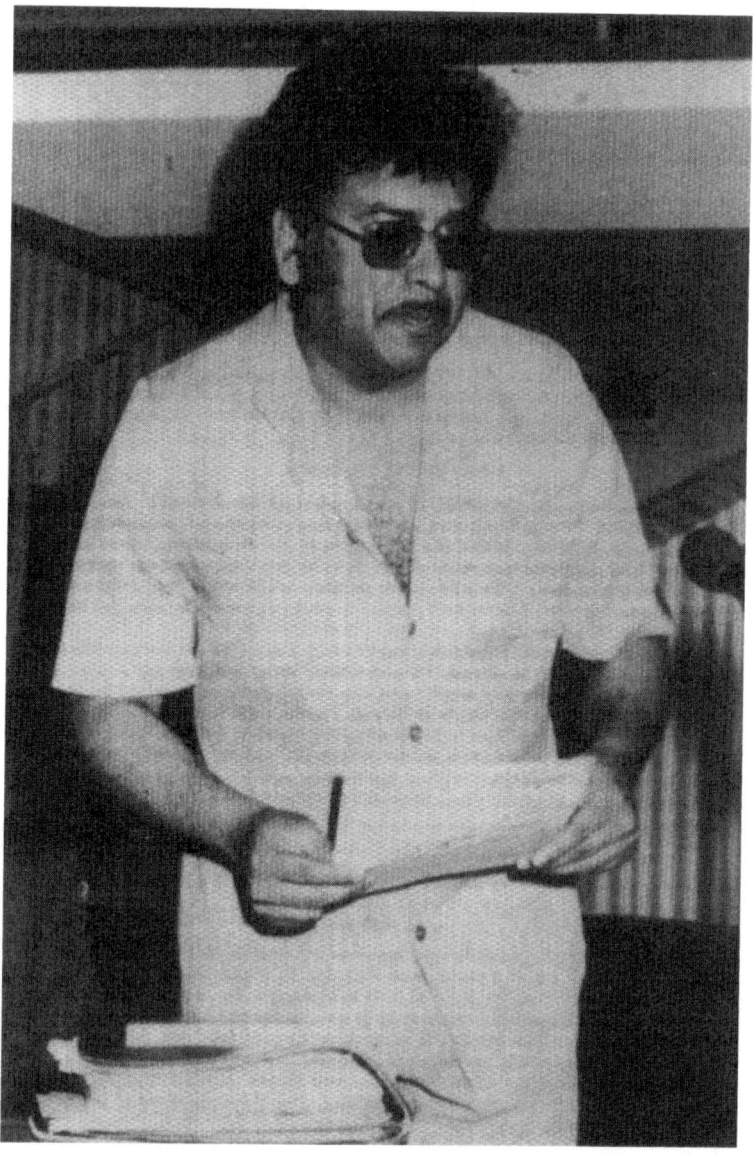

Rudy Narayan, Barrister-at-Law, who was instrumental in obtaining the release of Roy Sawh from prison in 1981

A very young Cassius Clay (Muhammed Ali) and a very, very young Roy Sawh

Many victories later

Len Dyke (Dyke and Dryden Ltd.) presenting Roy with a Caribbean Times Award

Roy Sawh making a point to Ashe Karim, Solicitor

From Where I Stand

L-R: Sam Springer MBE (former Mayor of Hackney) presenting a Caribbean Times Award to Clive Lloyd (former Captain of the Westindies Cricket Club)

Presenting a Caribbean Times cheque for £500 to Vernon Clements on behalf of O.S.C.A.R. (Organisation for Sickle Cell Anaemia Research)

Roy Sawh greeting Angela Bishop, wife of the late Maurice Bishop, Prime Minister of Grenada

Alf Dubs, Labour MP, at the offices of Hansib Publishing Ltd.

Roy Sawh receiving a trophy presented by justice House for his service to the community.
(L-R): Rudy Narayan (Vice Chairman of Black Rights), Arif Ali (Editor-in-Chief of Caribbean Times, Asian Times and African Times), Bernie Grant (Leader of Haringey Council), Lord Pitt of Hampstead and Canon Sebastian Charles of Westminster Abbey.

L.R: Arif Ali, Caribbean Times, Juliet Alexander, presenter of Ebony, BBC TV and Roy Sawh

David Waddington, Minister of State, Home Office at the Caribbean Times office.

In the words of Roy Sawh..

In an essay published in *Justice First*, a book edited by Lewis Donnelly, Roy Sawh put forward his thinking on Black Power. This essay was published in 1968 long before the emergence of violent confrontation on the streets between the police and the black community.

Black Power in Britain

Roy Sawh

All men are born free but it is always the white man who has given the black man his freedom. It is also an accepted fact among many people that it was the white man who, in the first place, enslaved the black man - that is why he always tells the world that he must give the black man his freedom. If one accepts the fact that to give back freedom one must have previously taken it away, then it is absurd to talk about making people free. In order to understand black power one must also understand how white power functions. There is no such thing as a black problem. What we are really talking about is a white problem; we are talking about the nuisance value of a race of people who, because of a delusion about the colour of their skin, are determined by words and deeds to reduce the rest of humanity to a level of animality from which they can never rise again. For too many years black people in different parts of the world have been suffering at the hands of white people. Wherever the black man may be, in Harlem, Angola, Vietnam, Rhodesia, Brixton or South Africa we draw the same water of affliction from the hands of the same man, the white man. We know that, with the exception of a few, the attitude of white people to black people all over the world is the same. We know that the only difference between the Ian Smiths and the Harold Wilsons of the white world is not a difference in principle but only a difference in tactics. We know that the quarrel between Smith and Wilson is not a quarrel between fascism and anti-fascism but a quarrel between frankness and hypocrisy within a fascist framework.

We have read the PEP report on racial discrimination, which now forms part of the history of our situation in this country, for who else would know how the white man's laws work? The 1965 Race Relations Act which was brought out for our welfare is the same Act which was used against black people. I myself was arrested four times under the Race Relations Act and charged with having made a speech allegedly inciting others to racial hatred. But when people like Enoch Powell and Duncan Sandys stood up and made speeches which were inflammatory enough to be condemned by the Archbishop of Canterbury, we found that these people were not arrested. And it is because of these factors that we realise that, perhaps inevitably, Smith and Wilson, Enoch Powell and Duncan Sandys merely reflect the Anglo-Saxon global attitude on racialism. We are aware of the plight of the black man in America, and in Canada Anglo-Saxon fascism has crystallised into European preferential migration and the anti-Asiatic Act. We know that in Australia the Anglo-Saxon civilisation has become enshrined in the white Australia policy, and that in South Africa it has escalated to the dizzy heights of apartheid. The English have always complained that apartheid has nothing to do with the English – it was the creation of the Dutch Boer, they say. But it is as well to remember that when the Nationalist Party was given its independence in 1910 the clause denying the black man the right to vote was actually written into the constitution, and it is because of this fact that today I define apartheid as the incapacity of the Dutch Boer to practise Anglo-Saxon racialism with the assured hypocrisy of the Anglo-Saxons themselves. We also know that in Rhodesia Anglo-Saxon fascism is rearing its head under UDI, and the white world, despite the protestations of kith and kin statements is applauding the rebels. If one were to pin-point the areas of the world where racial problems are most intense, the prominence of areas of Anglo-Saxon civilisation becomes obvious. The cultural mother of them all was only the last to close another chapter on legalised racism when her government introduced the Commonwealth Immigration Act of 1962, followed by the White Paper in 1965. With the recent Immigration Act of 1968, where black people have been denied the right of entry into this county just because of the colour of their skin, Britain has finally joined the ranks of other white power countries in legalising racism in the world.

These examples which I have given are all called by different names but in actual fact they can all be classified as examples of the white power structure. Because black people are powerless they could do nothing to prevent this kind of legislation. But had we some form of power, either political or economic, there is always the possibility that we could neutralise the situation if not overcome it. If the 'Vietcong' had not had some power the Americans would have been much more successful in imposing their way of life on the Vietnamese people. The war in Vietnam could be over tomorrow if the 'Vietcong' had two nuclear missiles, one aimed at New York and the other at California, and for the first time the American people would experience the horror that is an everyday experience for the Vietnamese. One can read in the newspaper reports on the fighting that 10,000 'Vietcong' have been killed but American losses were not severe, or 5,000 'Vietcong' killed, American losses not estimated, or again 2,000 'Vietcong' killed, some Americans missing. If one takes the total of those estimated dead between 1965 and 1968 according to the white man's propoganda, it would be shown that the Americans have killed twice the population of Vietnam already. I wonder whom they are really fighting.

Take a look at the map of Africa and you will find that all the islands off the coast of Africa belong to some white country, and even Hong Kong, which is 10,000 miles from Britain and so close to China, is a British Colony. If Britain really believes that power confers the right to dominate other countries, then when the day comes for China to rule the waves, I wonder if the British people will concede the Isle of Wight as a colony to the Chinese. The Opium Wars which resulted in the so-called "treaties" which were signed by China and the white powers of the West, reduced China to a nonentity. But, today, after the Chinese revolution, China is no longer a paper tiger but, in reality, a black panther which is being driven into a little corner.

The English are by no means the most beautiful race in the world, nor are they the ugliest. But I must confess that I find them a truly remarkable race. Their whole way of life is based on the Christian ethic and all their so-called 'morals' are determined by their own definitions. In this society, owing to the influence of Christianity, the concept of beauty is denoted by 'white' and ugly things are characterised as 'black'. When English newspapers and journals speak of anything as sinful they always say 'as black as sin'; similarly when they talk of those things which are pure and good they talk in terms of 'white'. Even when the newspapers describe the situation in Vietnam they say it looks very black. It is this kind of thinking which generates the belief that black power is associated with everything which is evil-killing, burning, violence and genocide. The domination of black peoples by white peoples is not called white power, but it is called by different names like slavery, indentured workers, colonials, Commonwealth immigrants, and now second-class citizens. But, in reality, this is what white power is all about. The world in which we live today is a world where white is right, and right is might, and might means power, and all the power in the world is controlled by white nations. The survival of black people in the world is controlled by white people whose fingers are constantly on the trigger. It is crystal clear to me that the world is divided between north and south, that is, black and white, and not east and west, as the masses of the world have hitherto been led to believe. Look at the map of Europe and you will see that to the north of Africa there is Europe, highly industrialised and white, but Africa remains underdeveloped and black. To the north of South America there is North America, highly industrialised and white, while South America remains underdeveloped and black. To the north of China there is the Soviet Union, highly industrialised and white; and this point one must make very clear to the world, that when Mr. Kosygin was in London he declared that the Soviet Union was a European power, and it is because of the Soviet attitude in foreign policies towards the Third World, towards the black countries, that in our definition the Soviet Union is a white power country.

Black intellectuals and students do not accept the situation of the world as it is today and it is for this reason that many of us have pledged ourselves to get together in trying to destroy the white political structure that keeps us in enslavement. The countries of the Third World which comprise the black nations can develop their own resources on a joint basis for the benefit of their own peoples rather than for the European. In this way they can develop their own democratic system, incorporating the welfare of their people and rejecting the white man's laws and his cultural imposition. According to the white man's history, nothing happened in Africa until Livingstone arrived, bringing with him to the so-called 'dark continent' the white Christian civilisation. In China the Chinese were asleep until Marco Polo arrived and said to the Chinese 'Wake up!' and only then, we are told, was life infused into the Chinese. In the Americas the same thing happened. If one happens to be a student of European history and of international history, one would have to accept that this whole concept of history has been distorted. White historians have justified the colonisation of the black countries by writing history in such a way as to exonerate the white power structures of their atrocities. But all this history that has been fed to us is nothing more than a lot of political goulash, and our contemporaries are, at last, disputing the validity of the white man's history of the black man. It is because of the white man's greed and lust that two world wars have already come about, and his inherent racialism may prompt a third. But if there is a fourth world war it will be fought with bows and arrows, for the white monster will have destroyed everything.

The concept of black power, which originated in a remote section of Alabama and became the slogan of many black people, has become a challenge to all the previous formulations of progressive and white radical partisans of the black people's movement. The new concept is contained in an analysis of the white imperialist societies of western Europe. Black power has been the object of virulent attacks by the capitalist-controlled and reactionary press. White pseudo-liberals have also attacked it, misrepresenting its essence, and some have failed to understand it and have thus distorted its content. In a little more than a year since the slogan was coined in Britain, many articles and comments on it have appeared in the leftist press, and discussions among intellectuals and leaders of various democratic and political movements have abounded. According to Leroy Bennett's definition, the idea of black power means the re-grouping of black people within their own political institutions and in terms of their own culture. The message of black power, in the language used by its advocate, is directed at the poor black people in the ghettoes of Notting Hill Gate, Brixton and Moss Side. Black power means the formation of bases of power from which the immigrants can establish coalitions with white people who have similar problems, but always on a basis of equality and not submission. The concept of black power also means the struggle to establish bases of political power instead of depending on the white man's political parties and white liberal left organisations. This, of course, will not be compatible with the ideas of the establishment. On the other hand, it is imperative that the white people organise parallel political bases in local communities through which, at the right moment, they can unite with the bases established by the immigrants. This, together with the tendency towards decentralisation, will encourage the collapse of the two-party system.

From Where I Stand

The political structure of this country is unable to satisfy the needs of the people. Integration is a subterfuge for maintaining white supremacy. And only when certain prerequisites are met, when the black man is nearly equal, will that equality mean anything, and will integration cease to be unilateral. Then integration at the new level will have a meaning. Until then we say no to integration. The appearance of the slogan 'Black Power' marks a new stage in the radicalisation of the immigrant masses which accords with the principle that the more any oppressed groups gain independence from the ruling class the more radical it becomes. Until now the capitalist bosses have been unable to contain and control the efforts of the black people to free themselves. Directly or indirectly, the capitalists and their flunkeys make all the rules and then persecute us under the same laws which were legislated to protect us. The Race Relations Act is a classical example and from it we know how the white man's laws operate. Owing to a series of historical, economic and religious factors the leaders of those so-called 'black organisations' have been acceptable leaders as far as the establishment is concerned – reformists and fair-weather liberals who know what they can and cannot do. I sincerely hope that, as a consequence of the recent Commonwealth Immigration Act, all the black leaders of the immigrant communities in this country will rally to the call to unity and Black Power. As regards organisation, the trend towards Black Power is in its early stages of development. The various groups and leaders who advocate Black Power have still not defined their relationship with each other, nor have they joined in a single organisation, but they have grown numerically and are already stronger than any other previous movement. Ideologically and politically Black Power is still in the process of development. Discussions and debates show that its advocates are still in the process of outlining and polishing, making their ideas clearer and more concrete, while their inclination towards the left and towards increased militancy is undeniable. The concept of Black Power already embraces the ideas of internationalism and anti-imperialism. Many leaders of Black Power groups have made statements of solidarity with the peoples of Africa, Asia, Arabia and Latin America in their fight against colonialism and neo-colonialism. We have condemned the war in Vietnam, terming it a racist war and how right our conclusion is when one asks oneself whether the Americans would go to South Africa to kill white people so as to enable my black brothers to be free. I do hope that those of our white blood brothers who really want to help will never even try to define Black Power for us because as members of the human race we reserve the right.

The most important aspect of Black Power is power. Frantz Fanon in his book *The Wretched of the Earth* makes this very clear:

"In a world where oppression is maintained from above it is only possible to liquidate it with violence from below."

Today the colour line is equated with the class line. Today, two out of three people in the world are dying of starvation. The two who are dying happen to be black people and the one who is not starving, be he capitalist, worker, peasant or priest, happens to be white. Workers are no longer workers, they have become black and white; a white worker employed with a coloured worker wants to create an aristocracy of labour, and when this condition is not met he goes on strike. White first and worker afterwards, he would rather make a pact with his kith and kin capitalist exploiter and go to distant lands with guns, bayonets and napalm to decimate, rob and rape the workers and peasants of other races to whom he feels superior. Even communists are no longer communists; they also have become coloured and white.

The white liberal believes in justice, equality and liberty, as long as these remain within the realm of abstraction. He believes in the fruits of revolution but disapproves of the revolution that brings them about; he cherishes the omelette but not the cracking of the eggs; he is an internationalist when it comes to theories but a white man when it comes to crunch; and the frightening thing is that here one is dealing with a man whose racialism is unconscious and who confuses intellectual masturbation with racial reality. We may not like this picture but it is a picture of the world in which we live, of a world in which the conflict between capitalist and worker is admittedly real, but one in which the polarisation of the world into black and white is even more real. Under these conditions no black man in his right mind can be expected to carry innocence to the point of believing that he can seek to sustain durable power outside the bounds of the black camp. Besides, to seek economic power within the existing white structures could only mean a replacement of the exploitation of black by white by the exploitation of black by black, a mere displacement of colour discrimination by class discrimination. Since our objective is the annihilation of oppression, not the butchery of colour, the only way the black man can get real power is by smashing the system which incubates the exploitation of the black. If he cannot smash it from within he must set in motion an international revolutionary force which will do the same job from without. The black man has no choice today. Either he smashes that system with active power or the system will take advantage of his passive powerlessness and smash him.

So from the foregoing analysis black power can be defined as the totality of the economic, cultural, political and, if necessary, military power which the black peoples of the world must acquire in order to get the white oppressors off their backs.

Black Power in Britain

The Home Secretary in Britain has made a lot of declarations. Measures must be taken to ensure that racial violence now sweeping America does not occur in this country. The Home Secretary has not said that racial discrimination must be discontinued because it is evil, inhuman and immoral. He couldn't. To call racism immoral would be to call his own government immoral. It was this government which legislated racism in this country with the Commonwealth Immigration Act of 1968. The Home Secretary made no effort to prevent the importation of racial violence into this country when only the black man was the victim of this violence in the States. He made no effort to keep it out when the blacks were being lynched and their little children bombed in churches. That was not violence worthy of prevention. But now that the tide of revolution is turning and the white man is suddenly becoming the victim of race violence, the Home Secretary wants to prevent violence. When the white backlash seized the whole of America like a plague and swept the fascist Reagan into power in California, there was no talk of preventing it in Britain. But when the tornado of black power begins to rage the Home Secretary wants emergency measures to prevent it. The implication is that he is not interested in stopping white violence, which has always been here. What he wants to prevent is black defence. The question is, can he prevent it?

Even if he could perform this miracle he is not going about it in the right way. How could he prevent the American type of racial explosion when he is repeating the mistakes of America?

For too many years the American white administration based their complacent attitude towards the racial problem on the historical assumption that the minority never resorts to violence. Today they are paying for it, the Home Secretary is limiting immigration to Britain while Enoch Powell is even preaching complete deportation. The assumption is that the less the number of blacks, the less likely are they to resort to violence. This is a wild dream – black power is not a quantitative entity, it is qualitative. Black Power is not a number, it is a degree of anger which the oppressed black man feels inside. It takes a single match-stick to burn London down; it takes one angry black man to light that match. Black Power is a revolutionary movement of black people. The smaller the number of people involved the more secure the movement. The black man is hitting out because he has been pushed to the limit where he can no longer breathe. To live, he has to breathe.

No Home Secretary, Labour or Tory, can stop him burning down the social system organised to enslave him. The present Home Secretary has done nothing to assuage this black indignation. On the contrary what we see in this country is the police hounding plain-speaking black leaders on one hand, and the press using the sign of imagery to slander them as pimps, drug addicts and thieves on the other. With this they hope to denigrate the black leaders in the eyes of their followers. The British should learn from the American scene, because the Americans tried to do the same thing and they failed. What they see is the white police kicking down the black militants and arresting them for assaulting the police. The idea is to dampen their spirits with handcuffs and a gruelling sentence in jail. America tried it too and only succeeded in extending the black revolution in the jailhouse when the passive negro prisoners of yesterday were converted to active participation in the revolution. What we see is middle-class so-called black leadership and sophisticated, lah-dee-dah organisations being forged and imposed on the black masses of Britain and given recognition as black mouthpieces. The trick is that with these black tentacles of white oppression the black masses will forever be lulled into the illusion that something is being done for them. America tried this too and found that the grass roots have a way of picking their own leadership, with New York, Detroit, Watts and Cleveland to prove it.

Today in America white persons of power and State Governors are pleading with tears in their eyes to negotiate with this real black leadership, only to find that this leadership, thanks to the recklessness of the police, has long been driven underground far beyond the reach of white negotiators. The white press that wanted them dismissed as hoodlums now pleads for a second opportunity to eat their words. But the invisible black leadership prefers to remain invisible. They have learned, underground, that the only way to remain invincible is to remain invisible. What use is press limelight, when a single cry of 'Burn, baby, burn', can set a whole city ablaze? Press prominence is paper power; grass roots power is real and this is called Black Power. What we see now in Britain is Stokely Carmichael being asked never to return. The logic is that once you have got rid of Stokely, you have got rid of Black Power. America tried it too, only to discover that the best way to make a saint of Malcolm X was to get rid of him.

America learned, as Britain must learn, that it is futile to get rid of revolutionaries when the very situation which makes people revolutionary is left intact. There is a difference between a philosopher and his philosophy. Getting rid of one does not mean getting rid of the other. There is a difference between the revolutionary and the revolution. A revolutionary is not the revolution. He is only a tiny speck in the wind of revolution. There are many more specks besides.

What we see is a Britain where a Home Secretary is talking about legislating against racial discrimination. The presumption is that legislation is a cure for racism. America tried it too and has since learned that legislating against racism is as effective as legislating against syphilis. Britain must wake up to the realisation that what she is dealing with here is a terrible man-eating disease which must be destroyed at once, or she will be destroyed by it. The question is, is it already too late?

We believe that the attitude of the white man is an attitude which is a collective attitude in Britain. This attitude ignores the basic factor of history. Every English person in England is an immigrant. It is arrant impertinence that one immigrant should demand entry as a favour from another. Every time a black man opens his mouth in protest, the white man comes out with the same question, 'Why don't you go back where you came from?' This attitude is based on a presumption. The presumption is that the black man is here by his own choice. This is an historical lie. The black man is no more responsible for being here than the cockney is responsible for being in Bermondsey. The black man here is only a speck in the wind of history. It was the Englishman who set that wind in motion.

Had the Russians colonised Africa, the black man would have been in Russia today. Had the Chinese raped Africa and Asia as the British did and still do, the black man would be flooding China today. No, we are not here of our own choosing. We do not enjoy slotting machines for heat, we do not enjoy the tyranny of landladies, we do not enjoy the taunts and insults of teddy-boys hiding in police uniforms. We do not enjoy seeing our beautiful black sisters on their hands and knees scrubbing the passage-ways of tube stations for ungrateful white people. We do not enjoy the agony in the eyes of those black girls when they look up and see their intellectual inferiors strolling by in jollity and affluence simply because they happen to be white girls. Every crack of a white stiletto on those platforms is a stab in the heart of a black girl who waits on her knees, mop in hand for the female members of the master race to sail by in jewels and diamonds which were stolen from the blacks. We do not enjoy our talented actresses and actors starving in a community which claims to be more racially adjusted than a Poitier-producing America. We do not enjoy seeing the political Baldwins of Britain being forced out of existence simply because they dare write the truth. We do not enjoy being black in a white-controlled Britain. No, we have not come here of our own choice. The white man came to us first. He came to our country and gave birth to a history which has brought black and white together. To date, that history has been a one-sided economic equation. We are here to balance that equation. It was the slavery of the black man that provided the capital for the industrial revolution of the West. It was black sweat that built the white civilisation. It was the flow of black blood that saved Britain in her world wars just as the same black blood is saving America in Vietnam. It was the exploitation of black lands which made Britain great; black essence has for centuries been the pulse, life and blood of white people on this isle. If the accumulated wealth of Britain is shared among the black immigrants here Britain will still be a long way indebted to her black benefactors. Yet we are expected to be grateful for partaking of the mere crumbs which fall from the table of our debtors. When the black man from the Caribbean plays his calypso records white neighbours cry out against the black invasion of white culture. The entire white state machinery is set in motion to acculturate this unfortunate black man. Commissions are set up and the help of the mighty BBC is enlisted to assimilate this uncultured black fellow, but when a white man from Britain goes to Zimbabwe not only will he insist on changing the name of the place to Rhodesia, he goes even further to preclude the native black man from having a say in the administration of his own soil until he learns the language and the administrative peculiarities of the white refugee. Isn't that the limit? We demand our cultural integrity as black people everywhere and warn parent and school management in this country to spare the psychological development of our school-children by never referring to them again as lowerers of standards.

On Violence

We do not advocate violence, but we believe that the only way to neutralise violence is to oppose it with violence. We are no initiators of violence, but if a white man lays his hands on one of us we will regard it as an open declaration of war on all of us. We do not believe in racial arrogance but we have plenty of racial pride. If the white man, whose record of racial arrogance has infuriated people all over the world, wants to stand between us and the modicum of pride which is ours we will ask him to get out of the way. If the white man does not want his cinema in flames there will be no more 'Africa Addios'. The white man will be well advised to keep to his bowler while I keep to my dhoti. If he insists on calling me a savage, I may not bother calling him a savage in return but I might be persuaded to show him how a real savage behaves. And then, no doubt, he would be in good company.

We are willing to accept that good white people exist, but we must say no when we are asked to let the existence of exceptions distract us from our task. When a man has a problem, he concentrates on the problem and not on the exceptions. When a man's house is on fire, and sees his bedroom on fire, his sitting-room on fire, but his kitchen is not on fire, what is he to do? – not raise a fire-alarm because there is an exception in the kitchen? Of course, it is laughable, but this is the kind of logic our white liberal friends expect of us. They want us to giggle when it doesn't tickle and scratch where it doesn't itch. The time for that is over. This is a new era, the era of Black Power. We have brought this about, it is like water springing up from the bowels of the earth, it is like a well shattering open the surface of the earth. Before the water bursts into the open it does not know which course it is going to take but once on top there is only one way for it to go, the way to the south. Once on the move, there is only one course the water must run, the way to the sea. So it is with the black revolution; it is now on the move. There is only one way for it to go, that is the way to total liberation. All we can do is shorten the journey to the end. What we must do is slash open a revolutionary canal which will quicken our tidal move to liberation. Whether this will mean a swim through a tidal wave of blood no longer depends on us. All we know is that we have to move, and move we must. All we can see is that we have a job to to do and we must do it quickly, and the only way to construct a canal is to cut away every obstruction in its path. We believe that the time has come when black people must stand up and be counted. This is the only way for black people not only in Britain but all over the world since this is an international problem which has been organised by racists on an international scale. We believe that Black Power can only be achieved by the consciousness of black people in the Third World.

The concept of Black Power, which originated in a remote section of Alabama and became the slogan of many black people, has become a challenge to all the previous formulations of progressive and white radical partisans of the black people's movement. The new concept is contained in an analysis of the white imperialist societies of Western Europe. Black Power has been the object of virulent attacks by the capitalist-controlled and reactionary press. White pseudo-liberals have also attacked it, misrepresenting its essence, and some have failed to understand it and have thus distorted its content. In a little more than a year since the slogan was coined in Britain, many articles and comments on it have appeared in the leftist press, and discussions among intellectuals and leaders of various democratic and political movements have abounded. According to Leroy Bennett's definition, the idea of Black Power means the re-grouping of black people within their own political institutions and in terms of their own culture.

The message of Black Power, in the language used by its advocate, is directed at the poor black people in the ghettoes of Notting Hill Gate, Brixton and Moss Side. Black power means the formation of bases of power from which the immigrants can establish coalitions with white people who have similar problems, but always on a basis of equality and not submission. The concept of black power also means the struggle to establish bases of political power instead of depending on the white man's political parties and white liberal left organisations. This, of course, will not be compatible with the ideas of the establishment. On the other hand, it is imperative that the white people organise parallel political bases in local communities through which, at the right moment, they can unite with the bases established by the immigrants. This, together with the tendency towards decentralisation, will encourage the collapse of the two-party system.

EPILOGUE

BY DR DAVID DABYDEEN

Looking back over his three decades in Britain, what does Roy remember most about the experience which he would define as particularly "black"?

"We came with innocent dreams and expectations of being treated as full citizens of our Motherland, a country which only recently we had fought for in the Second World War. But we were quickly and starkly disillusioned and shocked by white racist rejection and cruelty. My own personal experience, which is similar to that of many black people i.e. personal attacks, being spat on, refusal to be served in pubs, not being able to find suitable accommodation, and which symbolises our common and shared experience of Britain, is that of harassment and false imprisonment. Our daily struggle and anxiety was to find a job and somewhere secure to live, but these basic human efforts were constantly thwarted. As Sam Selvon, the Trinidadian novelist wrote in The Lonely Londoners 'after a while, we didn't even get on, we just wanted to get by!' I have personally spoken out and acted, in my own way, against the structure of racist oppression. Because of that challenge to the Empire, I have been subjected to several arrests and periods of imprisonment, even though Britain boasts of not having a tradition of political imprisonment."

In 1968 Roy spent two weeks in Brixton prison for daring to speak out nakedly on white racism. In 1979, as a result of a police "fix", Roy was arrested for allegedly assaulting a white man who had attacked some Asian workers. Although it was clear that he was not directly involved in the affray, and in fact was nowhere near the scene of the violence his reputation as a Black Power advocate was the undeniable reason for his arrest. It was a gross miscarriage of white justice. Roy was sentenced to three years imprisonment, but thanks to the brilliant advocacy of Rudy Narayan, he was released after three months. Upon seeking compensation for the period spent in jail the Appeal Court Judges made the astonishing and unprecedented declaration that, "the three months will be held in credit should Mr. Sawh ever find himself before these courts again".

Roy remains proud of the humble efforts he has made over the years to contribute to the struggle for civil rights in Britain, and in spite of the actions of the authorities, he remains committed to his original principles. He continues to work for the black community, work which is being increasingly recognised but which can only be fully rewarded when those principles he fights for are recognised in law and social action.

His latest venture has earned him a new reputation as one of Britain's leading catalysts in the campaign for a Bill of Rights. This campaign is being waged by Black Rights (U.K.) of which he is the Director. Its aim is to have the security of citizens enshrined in statute. Although certain of the rightness of the cause, experience has taught him to be pessimistic about a positive response from the Authorities.

"If the present situation continues vis-a-vis police/black relationships, and the denial of access to the corridors of power, I reluctantly predict a bleak and unfortunate future of riots and civil disorders; this will be regrettable not only for Britain, but also for the black community. The gruesome effect of such violence would be a white backlash, which the right wing element in this country would provoke and seize upon, to demand the repatriation of all black people. It is imperative that we begin now to devise intellectual, social and political strategies to thwart the possibilities of such a backlash, otherwise we will have lost. And history has taught us that we must not lose. Our strength lies in unity of purpose and action."